I WAS A WHITE SLAVE IN HARLEM

I WAS A WHITE SLAVE IN HARLEM

BY MARGO HOWARD-HOWARD

WITH ABBE MICHAELS

Four Walls Eight Windows

NEW YORK

Copyright © 1988 Robert Hesse

First edition published by:
Four Walls Eight Windows
Post Office Box 548
Village Station
New York, New York 10014

Library of Congress Cataloging-in-Publication Data

Howard-Howard, Margo, 1935–
    I was a white slave in Harlem/by Margo Howard-Howard.
      p. cm
    ISBN 0-941423-14-X (pbk.): $12.95
    1. Howard-Howard, Margo, 1935– 2. Impersonators, Female—
New York (N.Y.)—Biography. 3. Harlem (New York, N.Y.) I. Title.
HQ77.8.H68A3 1988   88-18047
306.7'43'0924—dc 19   CIP

Manufactured in the U.S.A.

I dedicate this book to the ladies who helped me in my recovery from drug addiction. They are the Sisters of the Congregation of the Blessed Handmaids of Mary, in Harlem. **—M.H.H.**

FOREWORD

I WANT to tell my story now, not to cause trouble or to start a scandal. It is because now the time is right.

In the 1950s, the world that I had been raised to honor and respect did a complete turnaround, and so did I.

As a child of privilege—an only son—I had been given every opportunity. It comes with being born to folks with the do-re-mi. I was christened Robert Henry John. I, who had a bloodline that included leading families on both sides of the Atlantic, now decided to call myself Margo—and for an extra goodie, to impress the squares, I tacked on two Howards. Thus I invented a drag queen extraordinaire: Margo Howard-Howard. I have lived with and as he/she for more than a quarter of a century, and I am going to share that life with you who are about to read my words.

I WAS A WHITE SLAVE IN HARLEM

THE DRUG KINGPIN
AND THE DRAG
QUEEN

1

I MET Leroy "Nicky" Barnes, the biggest, baddest, and most respected heroin dealer in the history of the drug world, at a girlfriend's apartment on the West Side in 1964. Leroy was then in his prime. When they finally put him away, some years later, they charged him with everything from failing to keep up on his mortgage payments to murdering people. Up to then he had never been prosecuted for a crime in his life.

Estella was a mixture of Latin and Scandinavian blood, very exotic. Leroy had been waiting for Estella at her place on 86th Street between West End Avenue and Riverside Drive when I rang the doorbell.

He answered the door, and very politely invited me in and asked me my name.

I said, "My name is Margo and I am Estella's friend. I shall await her arrival."

He told me Estella would be back after entertaining a trick in the neighborhood. Estella was not very choosy about her tricks. She wasn't quite up to the standards I set for myself. I had a British accent in those days and men were terribly charmed by that.

Leroy said to me, "What are you waiting for, a fix?"

"Yes I am," I admitted. "Why?"

He said, "I have anything you want."

"Really," I remarked. "How much is it going to cost?"

Leroy threw me a sly glance and said, "It won't cost you anything, baby. I like you."

"Really? I'd rather pay for it. I don't want to get involved."

First of all, I thought, he is a black male and, I presumed, heterosexual. I was a little apprehensive about that. After all, I had had nothing whatsoever to do with a gentleman of color before that time. However, I must add, Leroy was not quite black. As a matter of fact, his skin was the color of urine or, as we say uptown, he was a piss-colored trick baby.

I said again, "I don't want to get involved. I'd rather get what I can for fifty dollars."

"What's the matter, baby?"

"I don't want to talk about it."

Besides, my friend Estella had just come back.

She said, "Oh Margo, baby, how are you, darling? Hi, Leroy. Did you meet Margo?"

"Yes," he winked, "she's *fine*."

"She's a good friend of mine."

He said, "I want to give this broad anything she wants."

Estella looked at me. "Margo, I want to talk to you."

I said, "What is it, darling?"

She sidled up to me and said, "Margo, darling, let's go where we can chat." She excused herself to Leroy and pulled me into the bedroom.

Estella put her hand in mine and said, "Why don't you go with Leroy? Don't you know? He's one of the biggest drug dealers in town."

I said, "Darling, you know I'm a drag queen and not a real woman."

"That doesn't matter," she said. "Leroy is a freak! A certified freak!"

"Ooohhh." I was impressed. But . . . "I don't want to get involved. Not with my pure background. After all, I do have blue-blue eyes and white-white skin. I am quite comely and a redhead and, I might add, a natural redhead! I don't want to get involved. I just want to cop fifty dollars' worth of dope. I'm not feeling well."

Estella grimaced and pulled me back into the living room. Before I knew it, she blurted, "Leroy, this is funny. Margo is from very good people and she's embarrassed because she's not for real in the downtown department."

"That's all right," Leroy responded. "I like my women that way best, anyway." He removed a huge bundle of heroin from his jacket pocket and said, "Now, you and Margo get yourselves straight."

Estella grabbed my hand, the heroin, and a glass of water, and took me into her boudoir. We cooked it up without saying a word and injected it. I almost OD'd. I had never had such pure heroin in my life. It was exquisite!

I marched into the living room where Leroy was now comfortably sitting on a sky-blue velvet couch. I said, "I want to pay you, baby. I have to go."

"Where you going, mama?"

"I must go find my friend Geraldine at 32 West 74th Street, between Central Park West and Columbus Avenue." Smack always made my language so specific.

"How long you been using the stuff, baby?"

"Not long," I said. "I slipped into this accidentally through bad boyfriends and lovers and, oh, it's so sordid that I simply can't get into it. I'm deeply into heroin addiction and I can't help myself."

"I have all the heroin in the world. I like you very much."

"I just met you," I said.

"You're kind of grand," he said.

"I *am* grand," I said.

"I like that," he said.

"I'm very pleased that you do," I said.

"Will you come up to my place at Lenox Terrace?"

"What is Lenox Terrace?"

"Lenox Terrace is where all the nob-bobs in Harlem live."

I said, "What are nob-bobs?"

"That's the grand niggers. Where I live, the Buckingham, we have

3

a doorman, a twenty-four-hour doorman and elevator operator. In Penthouse D, we have Percy Sutton and the Reverend Adam Clayton Powell keeps his New York home there on the fifteenth floor."

"Oh, how very charming," I commented. "All the *riche* of the black world, it seems."

"Lenox Terrace is the grandest place you can live in New York," Leroy boasted. "It's a group of eight fifteen-story buildings maintained by doormen and elevator operators. Each apartment has its own terrace and view, beautiful views. It's real grand."

"Oh," I said, "you say if I come up to your flat in Lenox Terrace, at the Buckingham, you will bestow upon me a gratuity in heroin instead of cash." I thought, I'll turn a trick for heroin any day, greedy bitch that I am.

So we proceeded up to Lenox Avenue and 134th Street, the site of the still ever-so-charming Lenox Terrace apartment complex. We then proceeded to park his red sports car in the underground garage, went to the lift, and pressed the button. The door was indeed opened by an elevator operator. How grand. He called Leroy "Sir" and me "Ma'am." None of the apartment buildings on the Upper West Side had sophistication like this! In the mirrored lobby, we were greeted by our very own elevator operator, a dark man in uniform and cap. Very chic. He took us up to the seventh floor.

I said to myself, Boy, when they're grand, they're grand, these nob-bobs.

When we ascended to Leroy's floor, Leroy took my arm and escorted me to his apartment. He had converted 7A and 7B into a single apartment.

Swinging open the door, he said, "Do whatever you want, baby. Make yourself to home."

It was an old-time expression, "to home."

Surprisingly well decorated, the room had black, red, and gold Oriental carpeting, fine antique Louis XIV armchairs and couches, Regency tables, rich, gold-fringed curtains, brass lamps with satin lamp shades, marble end tables with assorted treasures atop them, exotic hanging plants, dried flowers in huge glass vases, and spectacular wall hangings from all over the world.

"Where did you get these things," I asked. "These are all authentic antiques."

He said, "Well, baby, I'm just dumb, but I have friends that have taste. And this pad has been decorated by a dyke I know who's a big decorator up here in Harlem for all the nob-bobs."

I decided to remove my shoes. I said, "What am I going to do? Where shall I go?"

"Go anywhere you want, baby." he said.

It was a very large apartment and I didn't know where to begin. I would say it had four plus four—eight rooms—very large rooms with nice high ceilings and spacious hallways. I noticed two balconies, one which faced south for a spectacular view of lower Manhattan and one which provided a gorgeous view of the Hudson River. I meandered into what must have been the main boudoir, a bit pretentious at that. A multicolored four-poster bed with silk curtains that surrounded it and a furry black bedspread was the highlight of this room. The carpet was incredibly shaggy and it felt good to prance around barefoot after taking off my springulator shoes, which I had on for over sixteen hours that day.

I entered the bathroom, which was all mirrors and chrome. A huge sunken bathtub with gold faucets looked tempting. To take a long leisurely bubble bath in there would certainly be a treat! I checked out the magnificent walk-in closet from there. To my astonishment, there were fabulous furs, gorgeous gowns, and everything else a woman could want. My eyes lit up. I held up an especially lovely, long yellow embroidered dress when Leroy walked in.

"Make yourself to home, baby."

I wasn't sure whether he was being sarcastic or generous.

"I apologize, Leroy, but I simply had to study these gowns more closely. They are astounding!"

"Margo, it's okay. Do you want to try it on?"

I looked at Leroy, who could not seem to take his eyes off me. "Go on," he said again. "Make yourself to home."

"Very well," I stated. "I shall."

I took off my black linen sheath dress and was left standing in my black taffeta slip.

He said, "Take everything off, baby."

"Oh please," I said. "Let's lie down. I'll take care of business for you."

"Just a minute," he said.

He went into the pissoir and removed all of his clothing. He wasn't bad looking, and he was in his mid-forties. Good body, not fat, very light skin, and a big, big, huge cock.

What a girl has to go through for a couple of days' fix of heroin. But it was worth it. I would have had to work extra hard pounding the pavements to get the money to get pure stuff like this. This type of heroin was impossible to get on the street. He really had it made. I then proceeded to lie down on the bed.

Suddenly Leroy came over to lie next to me on the bed.

I said, "What is it that you want?"

He said, "I want everything and then some."

"Oh . . . oh. What are you going to give me in weight, baby?"

"You can have all the heroin you want."

"That's rather generous."

"Take off that slip."

"Wait a moment, please. Now, now, let's please not be vulgar."

"Do you speak French?"

"Oui, oui, of course. Yes I do. Why?"

"Well, I thought you were classy. Where did you go to school?"

"I went to very good Catholic schools."

"I can tell."

"You can?"

"Because you got class."

"Thank you," I responded, "Very observant of you to see this. Now what is it we're going to do here?"

I was quite firm. I'll do what I have to do for the heroin, I thought, because I am a drug addict and my soul is lost to the hypodermic needle and the injection of the heroin fix. I asked him if he used heroin and he said he did not.

"I thought so! Oh, you poison peddlers! You cause all the suffering that those poor street girls go though."

But, I was stuck. Very well, I thought to myself.

I removed the black taffeta slip, at least I think it was taffeta; it could have been satin, but it definitely was not cotton. It had lace on it. I had a tight panty girdle on where my penis was pushed up, so you would not see the shape of it. If you put your hand on it, you could not feel a thing. It's called a "deception." To deceive, you know.

Anyway, I lay down on the bed with the panty girdle still on alongside this man, New York's heroin king, the biggest supplier on the Eastern seaboard. By then, my future was fixed. Suddenly, Leroy started kissing me fiercely. He took his hands and pulled my panty girdle down to my ankles and onto the floor.

"Lay down, baby. I want you."

I was feeling all right, but a bit perturbed that he was so determinedly taking over my body. But he was the biggest heroin dealer on the East Coast, I kept reminding myself. That alone certainly qualified him to be my future husband.

I lay down on the bed completely nude, my exceedingly long hair falling freely upon the gigantic goose-feather pillows. I wore white pancake make-up, false eyelashes, both upper and lower, bright lipstick which was a dark cherry red called, I think, Victory Red, an Elizabeth Arden stick, the same lipstick my dear friend, the late Tallulah Brockman Bankhead, used to wear.

There I stood, nude to the world. Leroy slid his tongue down my throat, his hands all over my body, including where they should not have been for a man, where they should not have been for a supposed heterosexual gentleman.

He said, "Baby, I love your white ass."

"You just met me," I protested. "How can you make a declaration of love when we just met several hours ago and have not consummated any sexual activity thus far. And I still have not gotten my hands on all that heroin you promised me. I need another fix, by the way."

"Don't worry about nothing, baby. Open your legs. Rest assured, you'll get everything you want and need."

Like I said, what a girl has to go through—but I could not help it. I was severely addicted to heroin.

I then opened my legs and he had his hand on my penis.

"Get it hard, baby."

"I don't want to get anything hard," I said.

"Play everything by ear, Miss Margo. You know how it is. You just put two and two together. Miss Margo, I've got more smack in this apartment than you will ever need in your entire lifetime."

How Leroy knew the way to a woman's heart! He then darted his tongue into my mouth again, down my chin, down my neck, over my then-small tits, over my belly, onto my cock, past my cock, onto my balls, up my asshole, down my legs, to the bottom of my ankles, over my feet, turned me over, licked my body completely from head to toe—a real depraved lowlife of the first water.

"I want you to fuck me," he said.

"That costs extra. I am a lady. That costs extra, my dear."

"Anything you want," he agreed.

"I haven't seen a goddamn thing yet."

"You ain't come yet."

"Do I have to come to get my money?" I asked. "I don't know what's going on here. I am distraught, upset, and completely appalled at your vulgar behavior. I am, first and foremost, not only a drag queen, but a lady in deed and word."

Next we did all sorts of freakish acts which seemed to please and gratify him. It was clear he was satisfied. He left and came back with a paper bag which contained nothing but $100 bills.

He said, "Take any amount of money you want, baby."

Then he brought out a plastic bag of heroin, about a kilo's worth. It had not yet been cut. It was pure as pure can be.

He said, "Take anything you want. Take as much as you can and stay as long as it lasts."

I said, "Oh, how completely divine." I wanted to stay forever. It was then that Leroy offered me just that. He suggested I maintain my residence in Harlem for access to the best smack in town. After careful consideration and after reviewing the assets, I decided that it was not at all inconceivable—and that, as a matter of fact, he did have a beautiful body and a fine cock and was rather comely, and, furthermore, he had the distinction of being the biggest heroin dealer on the Eastern seaboard with an entire closet full of uncut heroin and several cases in the apartment containing mucho, mucho money—that I was now going to be a Harlem resident.

"Leroy," I implored, "will you please have some of this cut for me?"

"Wait a minute," he responded. "I'll get you one of my lieu-tenants."

"What is, pray tell, a lieutenant?"

"Well," he explained, "in the Harlem ring, we have our com-mander-in-chief, me, and our staff of so-called soldiers, who do the gof-ing, the running, and things like that. This is Willy."

"Hello, William. How are you?"

"My name Willy," he mumbled.

"I beg your pardon, William," I said. "What is it?"

"Hey, Leroy boss" Willy muttered, "she called me, uh, uh, William, and my name's Willy."

Leroy was stern: "You'll listen to whatever she calls you. If she calls you a black fag cocksucker, you better listen to what she says. This is *my* woman. And she's the boss lady."

It did not take much to detect, through my educated background, that Leroy was ever so charming and debonaire, but highly ignorant, and smart as a fox only when it came to money and the drug operations. He was not very literate, but could read and write, however, and did not like to read much except for an occasional New York *Daily News* or *Enquirer* gossip rag. He also had some of those degenerate magazines lying around, showing deviant men doing terrible things. Yet in the world of marketing drugs, he was well-respected and very, very wealthy.

At this point, I said to myself, "Well, Miss Margo, you are on your way out." I would probably overdose on heroin or kill myself or something. I was feeling that sort of grand malaise. I now realized what I had gotten myself into and what I had left behind.

9

ROOTS OF A DRAG QUEEN

2

MY FATHER was John Hesse, a younger son of William Hesse, third Marquis of Shropshire, and Mary Fitzallan-Howard. He came from a family of Hanoverian origin that voyaged to England with George I in 1714. The Hesses were hangers-on, and worked their way up into the English peerage under the first two German Georges. William's father died when he was nineteen and he then ascended to the title. He met Daddy's mother, my grandmother, Lady Mary Arabella Howard, of the leading English Catholic family. She was the daughter of the 13th Duke of Norfolk.

Lady Mary was a daughter of England's premier duke and earl as well as its earl marshal. She was also a Roman Catholic. Old Billy wisely converted to the Roman religion of his ancient ancestors. As children of dukes and marquises all have by right of birth a courtesy title, my father was Lord John Hesse. As a younger son, he had to make his own way in the world. However, his background helped, and his title looked good on a letterhead in the corporate community. He met Mummy—my mother— in 1910 at a ball in New York.

My mother, Alida Beekman Chanler, a great belle of old New York, was a bit of a blue stocking and "veddy, veddy" snobbish. She was born in 1888. She was a Victorian and had Victorian mores. Given her breeding and the period, she was a perfect young Edwardian lady. Do I dare criticize her? My mother's father was a real Yankee prig, anti-everything. When she married Daddy and was received into the Roman Catholic Church, her father never forgave her. He was Winthrop Chanler, a son of Caroline Astor. His wife, Margaret Van Courtland, was the last of that distinguished New York line of *patroons*. Her brother, Lewis S. Chanler, was New York's Lieutenant Governor from 1906 to 1908. Mummy's sister Meg, or Margaret, married Richard Aldrich of Boston, son of the poet Thomas Bailey Aldrich. Their late son Winthrop was U.S. Ambassador to the Court of Saint James. My good Lord, now in the 1980s they are all gone. But I have survived, and now prosper.

My nearest English kin is William, Marquis of Shropshire. He is closer family to me than the Duke of Norfolk, to whom I am also related. We have the same surname—Hesse. His daughter is currently being courted by Prince Edward, the Queen's son, the unmarried one. The Marquis specifically asked me, when he heard about this book, not to mention him. I told him that I was sorry, but he was part of my heritage.

This book may upset much of the English aristocracy. Not upset, exactly: ruffle feathers is more like it. I can hear them now. "Oh, why must he mention us in that damn thing." I think a little humility will make them stronger. After all, consider the Howard family, second in social precedence only to the royal family. Who are their ancestors? Numerous traitors. Half my forebears were executed for treason. They were always plotting against the crown. A few saints, but many sinners. A transvestite or two, too, besides me. Of course, I'm a drag queen; they were transvestites. They dressed in women's clothing for sexual excitement. I do it because I feel like it. And we had a few addicts in the family. One duchess died of too much liquid laudanum. Mary Todd Lincoln took it, too. She used to drink a quart a day for her nerves.

It doesn't matter who or what you are, or where you are. We're all susceptible to weakness. Heroin is a terrible weakness, and I had such little self-worth at the time I was a full-fledged addict, a slave to the stuff, that it is only now I am realizing my full potential as a human being. What an asshole I was. But it's never too late to redeem oneself.

12

GROWING UP ABSURD

3

GROWING *Up Absurd* was a title used by Paul Goodman over twenty years ago. I only wish I had come up with it first. After all, I have all that heritage to own up to . . . It was not easy growing up, particularly because my mother was nearly fifty when I was born. She hadn't had a child in eighteen years. My four older sisters came in steady succession: Eleanor (born 1912); Claire (1914); Virginia (1915); and Annabelle (1918). When my parents moved to Singapore after Daddy got a big promotion, no one expected that Mummy would be with child again. My sisters, who served me more as aunts, had stayed behind with Granny in her lovely Gramercy Park residence, preparing for their college studies. When they were informed of my birth, all four along with Granny crossed the Pacific in a journey that took a total of fourteen days. After 20,000 miles on the P & O line, they figured they might as well stay in Singapore for at least three months.

The city of Singapore takes up about less than ten percent of the island and is separated by the Strait of Malacca. Our home was on St. Patrick's Road, just off the strait. Our house was very large, featuring a formidable party room upstairs with a roof that would open automatically in just under ten minutes. Since the humidity was often staggering, this was a lovely way to cool our home in the absence of air conditioning. Ceiling fans and individual fans carried by the servants also cooled us.

Allow me a moment of remembrance of things past as I, the five-year-old Robert, wander into the huge immaculate kitchen of our Asian abode in search of a sweet.

I could smell the succulent odor of European fare being prepared by our wonderful Chinese chef: juicy roast beef, sweet and yummy Yorkshire pudding, tender lamb chops, fresh peas, and creamy potatoes. Imagine such food in that awful heat! Our servants were plentiful and rather well paid for the time, even if they were more used to the sweltering temperature and had not a clue on how to prepare a cold platter. The servants were Indian, Malay, and Chinese, and there was not a minute when one was not right by my side, willing to assist me in every detail of my life. Even to utilize the *pissoir*, a young Indian boy would accompany me and wait outside the door until I was through. Well, this same boy caused quite a scandal as the culprit in a scene with yours truly.

I was lurking about mischievously and, of course, being followed by the boy. What neither he nor I knew was that Granny was also following my path. I tiptoed past the huge cast-iron stove which was constantly burning under huge pots of soup and other delights. As I reached into a cupboard to claim my prize, the young Indian touched my derrière. I was flabbergasted not by this gesture, which I had presumed to be nothing more than a friendly pat, but by the sight of Granny, who was so upset over the Indian boy's prank that she grabbed the boy's hand and placed it on the stove. He screamed and cried until his mother, who was polishing the silver in the dining room, came running. She, who was once my governess, immediately called upon the magistrate to arrest my grandmother. She was in hysterics: "Why, you have maimed the child's hand for life!" As my grandmother and the Indian woman argued it out, help was on its way. It strikes me now as odd that rather than rush an ambulance over to aid the ailing boy, his mother had called upon the authorities! When the police officer arrived, he questioned Granny.

He said, "Mrs. Chanler, I have a paper to serve you. A native woman has accused you of injuring her son and you must appear before a magistrate. What day is convenient for you?"

"Any day," she calmly replied. "How about tomorrow?"

The boy and his mother studied the scene in outraged silence.

They knew how very powerless they were as common servants and, to make matters worse, non-Europeans.

The court ordeal was even more absurd. Granny admitted what she had done and the judge said, "I have had the distinction of meeting your husband when I was last in Warsaw and he was U.S. Ambassador at the time. It is indeed a pleasure to make your acquaintance, Mrs. Chanler. The court finds you guilty of no criminal offense."

Ah, the days of British colonial imperialism! The Indian mother and son went back to their homeland, never to work in Singapore again.

My grandmother certainly was a tyrant and would create trouble any way she could. Each morning, when my father would call for a rickshaw (which would take him downtown in fifteen minutes flat), my grandmother would hail another rickshaw and call, "Follow that rickshaw, coolie, but don't get too close!" Later she'd report to my mother: "Alida, your husband is a womanizer. All of those chi-chi Eurasian women that work with him he has affairs with. I know."

Now, my father was a very liberal man. He was one of the first in the Orient to hire natives in a bank. Known as chi-chis, they were Eurasian girls with college degrees who could find no work and therefore wasted their skills as typists, bank tellers, and secretaries.

Granny was suspicious of other aspects of my father's business practices as well. It seemes to me she was constantly scheming, a Lucy Ricardo of her time, most probably because she was bored and had nothing better to do.

One day when Daddy was on his way to meet Mr. Lee, a Chinaman and the owner of one of the largest buildings in Singapore, Granny decided to hail another rickshaw and follow. The building was the site of apartment houses, offices, a hotel, and a fabulous roof garden/nightclub. It must have cost a fortune to insure. Granny walked in just as the owner was counting out to Daddy quite a large pile of English bills. Granny struck Daddy's hand with her walking stick and shouted, "Aaah! Corruption! English corruption in the Orient! Taking bribes!" As the grand dame led my shocked father out of the building, she continued her charade: "Whoremaster! Thief! Corrupter! Bribe master! I caught you in the act!"

Poor Daddy, the gentleman that he was, would say or do nothing. His friends and business associates would remark, "John, your mother-in-law, what a demon she is! Every time she comes to the colony she drives you crazy and puts you through hell!" My father would reply, "Well, I can not say anything about that lady. She is my mother-in-law and it would not be gentlemanly to speak of her in that way. As a Christian, it's one of my crosses to bear."

I have to wonder how my father put up with all her madness. I never once heard him complain to my mother about her, nor anyone else for that matter. My father was one of those saintly types that you would like to see, just for the hell of it, fly into a rage.

My mother was quite the opposite. She was opinionated and outspoken. I loved my mother wholly, but because I knew her much longer than I knew my father, I probably have a much more realistic portrait of her.

My mother was quite confident managing her money; never an extravagant woman, she had a fine sense of dressing—later, she never wore synthetics (even her stockings were imported from England). She was a very strong-willed lady and very demanding—it was always "my money," "my house," and "my ideas" with her. We had to go by her rules. It was no wonder she was one of the early suffragettes.

Being the convinced Catholic convert that she was, she thought I was sent by God to her in her old age, as if she were Saint Elizabeth. (Saint Elizabeth, the mother of John the Baptist, had her child when she was fifty.) Not only did she reckon my birth was a sign from God, but she thought it was inevitable, being that I was the only male of her offspring, that I should become a priest.

Therefore, I had a very Catholic education. I was sent to Portsmouth Priory, the prep school run by the English chapter of the Benedictine monks in Portsmouth, Rhode Island. It was beautifully situated right on the ocean, adjoining Newport. I remained there for my secondary schooling as well and then was accepted at Georgetown University. In a large way, my youth was consistently under the influence of Catholic propagandists.

The happiest moments of my life were between the ages of five and seven, the time that Daddy spent teaching me the ways of Catholicism. Suddenly, it became clear to me who God was and why God made me. The answer: God made me to love him and to serve him. At seven, I received my first Holy Communion. At that time, I sincerely believed in the spirit of the Holy Ghost. I asked my father how could a piece of bread have so much meaning? "Symbolic," he said. It was all so symbolic.

Daddy went on: "A priest is one of God's servants and he has the right and the power to consecrate."

Anything Daddy said I took to heart. I loved him very much. He was very warm and giving, unlike my mother, who, in reality, was a cold fish. Daddy found time out of his busy schedule to take me on various excursions. Once we took a ride to see the snake farms in Pen Yang. Dancing cobras were trained to move to the sound of flutes, tails rising and tongues lashing out, the stuff of Hollywood movies.

Meanwhile, Mother stayed at home to play bridge with the other society ladies in Singapore, the wives of the French, American, and English businessmen. Many major corporations had branch offices in Singapore as well as in Hong Kong and Shanghai.

My mother was not a demonstrative person. An occasional peck on the cheek at birthdays and other celebrations was it. Early in the evening, around eight, my father would tuck me in and give me a kiss goodnight. My mother was reserved and did not approve of displays of affection. She was very reserved. In fact, she accused me of making a fool of myself by crying at my friend's mother's funeral once.

When I was sixteen, the priest finally confided to my mother that I did not have the vocation.

Nevertheless, she pushed on. "I want him to be a priest."

The priest was persistent. "Lady Hesse, he simply does not have the vocation."

At least he was honest. And a good priest.

Our years in Singapore passed quickly. I was carefree and happy, seduced by an easy and comfortable existence. War was in the air, but I was too young to begin to understand the danger and horror that lay ahead. However, one day Daddy decided that we would have to vacate our beautiful home. In what seemed like just a few hours, we had packed

Mother's jewelry and were on a queue to board a plane. It was the last plane leaving Singapore before all hell would break loose. People were pushing and shoving each other to make sure to win a place on board, but we, as V.I.P.'s, had seats for three.

Mummy was clutching my hand firmly, and determinedly standing our ground. Meanwhile, Daddy was checking out the scene and we could see the somber expression on his face. He turned to Mummy and said, "Alida, there are women and children behind us in the queue. As a gentleman, I cannot board the plane ahead of them. I shall let a lady take my place. I'll just be interned."

Mummy, of course, became hysterical. "What do you mean? They'll kill you! Please, come with us!"

Mummy begged Daddy to come, but he insisted on staying behind. Strangers were awed by his gallant gesture, but Mummy and I froze. As we climbed the stairs of the plane with fear, we looked behind and tried to wave to Daddy. The crowd was pushing us forward, however, and I caught one small glimpse of my father. He appeared so tiny from this distance, and I can remember waving to him as I swallowed all my breath to keep myself from crying. Then I suddenly became nonchalant. This was a pattern which would establish itself in the future. Hide the pain, keep it inside, and move on to the next thing.

LEAVING SINGAPORE

4

AS MUMMY and I flew off on the last plane from Singapore, once her hysteria was under control, she assured me all would be well, as she always had faith in her U.S. citizenship. She was convinced that representatives of the United States of America would look after her interests and give all the aid they could while evacuating their people.

Before we caught the neutral Swedish ship, we spent time in Bombay, getting ripped off by the natives who took advantage of our desperate situation. A particular friend of my mother's, Emma Smalley, had been killed on an American ship, the S.S. *President Taft*, so we were not taking any chances. My mother was so distraught that she absolutely refused to sail on an English or American ship. I remember seeing the Japanese submarines skimming the surface of the ocean, a constant warning.

We next landed in the city then named Batavia, on the island of Java in the Dutch East Indies (known today as Jakarta, Indonesia). We immediately went to the U.S. Consul General's office. What a scene this was: Clerks and secretaries were burning files on the lawns. There were about seventy-five to eighty-five U.S. citizens—all women and children— milling about. Naturally, there was pandemonium. The Japs were hours away. All asked for protection from their government. What was so very disturbing to Mummy and the other ladies was the dastardly, lowly, cowardly conduct of the Consul General of the U.S.A. He was in a great panic and fled with his wife saying, "No screaming! I can't help you! I must get out as I have vital information on the Far East that Washington needs." The consular clerks advised us to report to the Dutch police office on the waterfront.

Calls were made to the Dutch, and lorries or trucks were provided to take us all to several Allied ships in the harbor for evacuation. A kindly Dutch officer, Colonel Hans Van Bracken, said to Mummy, "Not to worry, *meine Frau*. I will see to it that you and the other ladies with their children are not caught by the Japs."

We were then taken to the docks. There was an English naval ship at the pier. The ship was the H.M.S. *Cornwall*. Well, we, the civilian enemies of the oncoming Imperial Japanese Army, were taken aboard ship. The captain and commander of the ship, C. Temple Bradshaw, was a middle-aged gentleman of true stalwart British tradition. He was quite gallant and warm to the European and American female refugees. Mummy and I were on the foredeck and I can recall to this day her words to Commander Bradshaw: "Sir, I am Lady John Hesse, a woman with an English courtesy title by marriage, but a citizen of the republic of the United States of America, first and foremost. A citizenship which I maintain to this day. For the first time in my life, I must say that I, who am so very proud of my family's service to my nation, am ashamed over the conduct of one of my country's representatives."

He said, "What is wrong with your nation's Consul, Lady Hesse?"

"It's so very difficult for me to put in words, Commander. But I must state what transpired at the U.S. Consulate. The Consul fled without giving aid or succor to the American women and children. I do see, sir, that you have received him on board ship."

"What do you say, m'lady?"

"I say what I have said, sir, and that can be attested to by dozens of witnesses."

After the Commander heard the true episode of the honorable Consul's behavior, he ordered him—I forget his name now—to disembark.

The Consul General to Batavia for the Republic of the United States of America shouted loudly, "Sir, I have important information for my government to impart."

"Well, Mr. Consul," Commander Bradshaw said, "I suggest you give it to your wife or aides, as I have bona fide testimony regarding your questionable conduct as an official of the U.S. of A. My disgust will not be further articulated for now, as there are females present. However, I give you two minutes to disembark or I will personally kick your ass off my ship."

As Commander Bradshaw removed the pistol from his holster, the Consul disembarked posthaste and suffered just as cruel and harsh an internment as did the thousands of other foreign civilians living in the East whose governments were at war with Japan and who were so unlucky as not to leave by the time Asia was overrun. The ship left as quickly as the Consul. An officer explained the ship's emergency rules to the refugees. As females with many young children, we were to have the sailors' quarters and remain below deck until our destination, Colombo, Ceylon. I remember I was so angry because I was given a cot to sleep on and not a hammock. As a precocious and spoiled child, as well as a know-it-all, I wanted to have my own way. I was a seven-year-old brat who never did a damn thing I was asked. Rather, if I was told not to do such and such, I would make it my business to do exactly the such and such. This was little me. This is me now in my prime.

I will not go into child behavior patterns or what a lack of discipline can do at such a period in a boy's life when rules must be applied very strictly. Rather, let me relate how my life was traumatized on that English ship. Must I blame sailors, Englishmen, or in my sensible madness, Japan, Japan, Japan? Well, let me take you below deck again as we sailed far into the night.

Everyone was emotionally exhausted. After all, their men were left behind to face . . . what? All collapsed to their allotted sleeping spaces. My mother said, "Go to the toilet and then, if you wake up, do not wander. Stay by the cot and above all, remember, we are forbidden on deck as we may be attacked by enemy planes and could be injured or killed."

That's all I had to hear. Oh boy, how camp I was. I am sure that word I did not know, but it was with that sort of feeling of adventure that I feigned sleep after waiting for enough time to go by in my oh-so-sharp devious seven-year-old head. I was an extra-curious, quite remarkable, oh-so-sweet little boy with an undetected touch of mischief and, like a method actor, I could and did put it over on any and all grown-ups. (My peers, however, saw through my charades.) Well, my timing was on perfect cue. Not a soul stirred. I was at liberty to take a tour of the ship. How full of myself I was feeling. Oh joy, I will be the one and only child to hit the deck and see the great guns, watch the ocean, and perhaps see the Big Dipper in the sky or, if I am extra lucky, see a shooting star.

I was rehearsing my lines to tell the other children. I certainly would rub the story of my tour on the forbidden deck right in. How they would envy me! I was looking forward to that, being a little megalomaniac even at that tender age.

After finally getting to the deck, I found most of the sailors asleep. I was seen by more than a few sailors who wore their "Hello, laddie" smiles. No one told me that I shouldn't be there. I hadn't run into an officer as yet.

What luck I had, being a child innocent and pure at the age of seven, until that fateful night, that is.

As I ventured on the deck, a sailor with a beard approached me. Later, on reading the transcript, I would find out that he was a thirty-year-old sailor named Albert Cookson of Leeds, England.

He said to me, "Hello there, laddie. Me name's Bertie and what is yours?"

"Sir," I said, "my name is Robert Chanler Hesse of Singapore."

"Well, what good manners you do have. A proper little gent, you calling me 'Sir' and all that. Were you born in the home country or over here?"

"I was born and live here," I replied, "but Mummy and Daddy had me back home three times." (Home being England to me then.)

"Oh, I see. Is your Dad with the Colonial Service or in business?"

"My father is a banker, sir. Daddy is home for two months' vacation leave every two years."

"I can't see how all them mucky mucks out there let their kiddies be brought up by black or chink heathens. It's not natural. I say, you are a stout-hearted top-drawer little boy coming up here like this, as well as a bit cheeky. But then I was and am cheeky myself. Tell you what, Bobby. I'm on watch in a few minutes. I go up into the crow's nest way up there," the sailor said and pointed it out to me. "I'll fetch a thermos of tea and let you watch with me, but we have to be a bit sly with the rules. I will show you a place to hide behind one of the ship's lifeboats."

He took me there and told me to wait until I counted to one hundred.

"Can you count that high?"

"Oh yes, sir!" I could barely contain my excitement.

"Now Bobby boy, you call me Bertie and that's an order as you are going to be in the Navy for a few hours and on duty. I am your senior officer. Do you know what that is?"

"I think so, Bertie. It's like a manager of one of the banks and his clerks. You're the boss for this watch job."

"Bright, sharp, and keen you are and know how to take orders. You called me Bertie right off after I gave the order. Now sailor, report to the crow's nest later after the count of one hundred. Oh yes, and another thing, do be sure that you are not seen and climb up as fast as you can."

I was so thrilled. So innocent was I, pure of heart and mind. I knew when I was counting that I must be extra careful or this great adventure, this most exciting game that I have ever played, would not come about. After counting not only to 100, but with a count of ten more for good measure, I carefully looked about. It was quite late, a few minutes after midnight, and I saw that now it was my chance, for the area was clear of people. I got up there so fast. It was about two stories high up from the deck. Only Bertie was watching me.

He said, "Well seaman Bobby, I see you are a good observer. Now you sit down on that blanket. I must stand and watch the sea, but we can talk and do a few navy larks. You do want to do what all us blokes in His Majesty's navy do, don't you?"

"Oh yes, Bertie," I replied.

"Oh, good boy." He ran his hand through my hair. I did not think a thing about it. He gave me some tea from the thermos and asked all sorts of questions. He had his hand on my shoulder and patted me on the back.

Now on to the true saga of horror, the traumatic experience and emotional shock, both physical and mental, of a seven-year-old child of privilege who came from stock that just never mentioned the danger of advances from deviant older men.

"You say you're seven, boy. Well now, did you play with the coolies, kiddies your own age out there?"

"Oh, no, Bertie. They were never allowed to be with us European kids."

"Oh, yes. I see. Did you go to school out here?"

"No, I had a tutor, an English tutor. I am supposed to go to Stoneyhurst after my next birthday."

"Oh, yes, at home. That's the Catholic school. Oh, so you're not of the Church of England? No matter, it's all the same humdrum. Do you have any mates from Singapore on board? I noticed about three who looked your age."

"There are two, but Giles Stanhope is eleven."

"I bet he knows what his prick and bollocks are for or will know soon. Do you boys out here play with each other?"

I did not know what he meant. I knew the English working-class slang word "bollocks" meant "balls," but our class of children did not experiment sexually. We were far too sheltered with many servants in attendance, in some cases just to watch over us as we slept. I stood mute, not knowing what he was talking about. He then said, "Give us a kiss, Bobby."

Now this did not seem too odd at all. My father kissed me on the cheek every morning. So I kissed his hairy cheek.

He said, "I'll show you a Navy kiss."

"Oh, good," said I.

He said, "Open your mouth a bit."

I obliged and he put his tongue halfway in my mouth.

I started to laugh. "That's funny. It feels so strange."

"Ah, laddie, a pretty boy to me is better than any woman."

I still didn't know what he was talking about.

"Now Bobby, look how big my cock is."

He unbuttoned his flap and out popped a big hard-on. I had never seen an adult penis before and saw other boys my age on few occasions, only if we were pissing at a party and had to share a toilet bowl, and looking not out of interest for that matter. Oh boy, I had never seen a grown man's cock before.

"Well, laddie, that's eight-and-a-half inches. Feel it. Your own cock will be as big, maybe bigger when you grow up."

"Oh really?" I saw nothing wrong in touching it. I mean, I was so dumb.

"Oh, grab it harder," he demanded. "Give it a kiss."

Well, for being so innocent, I still had a feeling that it was not quite the thing to do.

"I would rather not, Bertie."

"Ah, Bobby, it's quite all right here. I'll suck your little bat here and see if you can get a hard-on."

I therefore received my first blow-job. However, it tickled and I laughed and did not get a hard-on.

"Now your turn," Bertie said.

"No, I would rather not. I did not say I would. You said you would to see if you could get it hard. I don't ever remember it hard."

He then said, "Well, laddie, you're not the first young boy I broke in, nor the youngest. I fucked me sister's boy, Rupert, when he was five."

Then he smacked me hard in the face. I was never slapped in my life until then. I started to cry.

He said, "All you gentry snobs are the same. Now shut up or I will knock you unconscious, then fuck you and toss you into the sea."

He smacked me again. "Understand me now."

"Please sir," I protested. I did not want to call him Bertie ever again. "Nobody has ever hit me before. Why? What did I do?"

"Never mind. Off with your trousers or you will get a proper good beating. He then unbuttoned my white linen short knee-length trousers and ordered me to step out of them. Quite bewildered I was, now standing in only my white knee-length stockings, white linen underpants, and white leather shoes. I was ever so confused and bewildered. A feeling of panic and fear of the unknown overcame me.

"Get yer draws off," he commanded.

I stood there, unable to move. A bit catatonic, I would say.

Then he grabbed my waistband and tore my underpants off. He pushed me to a blanket on the floor, face down and ass to the sky. He then put a lubricant on the opening of my anus with his finger and put that up there, too. The shock of this had my mind blank.

Next he said in a sadistic and rough, gravel-toned voice, "Now you're going to get a good hard fucking and I get another cherry and make another freak."

He sodomized me with such force. He rammed the whole penis in with one thrust. I actually saw nothing but blackness with shooting white stars before my eyes. I then became unconscious and fainted. However, in his lust, he had become careless with the sea watch and was caught in the act of sodomizing me. Bertie Cookson was sentenced to twenty-five years in His Majesty's gaol for his sins.

I recall nothing after that of what went on aboard ship. The ship's doctor, in his mercy, kept me sedated. I was roused from my sleep in a lovely house in Colombo.

One week later, Mummy said, "Bobby dear, you have been quite ill. We are in Ceylon on our way back to America and you had a nasty fall and have been unconscious for days. How do you feel now?"

I know she knew something of what had actually happened and did not want to discuss it at all. She was of that school of ladies who simply refused to deal with situations of emotional upheaval or anything that upset their apple cart. In other words, don't think rationally about an unpleasant event or subject and you will convince yourself it never happened.

We continued the journey toward the Americas. From Ceylon, we travelled to Chile, and up through South America by train, plane, and hired car. We crossed through Mexico and finally reached California. I cannot recall much of that part of the trip except for the fact that my mother was in a state of bewilderment over what I had been through and I was in a flux of confusion due to heavy medication. I suppose that was the idea. It was as if we were mere objects being pushed forcefully from one country to the next. Our survival instincts kept us alive and going, yet our emotions were distraught. Mummy had to depend on the hope of the future that our lives would be happy again eventually and that Daddy would be home soon with us. In the meantime, she wanted to depend on New York City to inspire and stimulate us enough to keep us from thinking too much about our current plight. When we arrived in New York, after our four-month trek, we subletted a gorgeous, twenty-room apartment from Mrs. Christian Herter, my mother's best friend, who was moving to California to witness the birth of her first grandchild. Christian Herter, her husband, was U.S. Secretary of State 1959–1961. Our address was 1010 Fifth Avenue, an elegant and proper place to begin our new life. Mummy kept talking of how "John would love the den" and "John would adore being so near the Metropolitan."

I attended an all-boy Catholic school called St. David's where highly specialized classes were taught in people's homes. Similar to the Montessori method of teaching used in other schools, we used blocks, pegs, and puzzles to build our minds, fitting shapes into holes and putting pieces of puzzles together to try to discover answers to questions. The idea of reaching and establishing independence at an early age was the main thrust of this learning approach. The experimental St. David's was declared an official institute of learning in 1950.

My British accent made me quite the outcast. Although I was crudely nicknamed "Limey," I was befriended by a few chums: Ernest (Ernie) Luckenbach; William (Billy) Carstares IV; and a South American boy named Armando DeCuvas who looked like a monkey. His grandfather was Antonio Patino—"The Tin Kingpin"—who had the largest tin exporting business in the world. Antonio's mother was a Throwbridge, from an old wealthy New York/Massachusetts family.

I had a restricted and sheltered childhood. It was almost like being in jail. I'd sometimes accompany my sisters on shopping sprees to Lord & Taylor's and B. Altman's. Our chauffeur-driven Bentley would pull up in front of the store and I, dressed most neatly in knickers and suspenders—it was absolutely essential that my shoes, cuff links, and belt buckle were polished to a shine—hand-in-hand with Annabelle, would choose a new outfit. The tailor would pin it up, the fit was customized, and it would suit me for perhaps the next six months until I'd have to go again to have another fitting as my build increased.

Toward the end of our stay on Fifth Avenue, tragedy struck, leaving our family with a giant gap that could never and would never be filled. We learned of Daddy's death.

I had never really understood why Daddy had given up his place in line. How could he have chosen to stay behind "as a gentleman" when the people he loved most in the world were beside him? Well, I later found out why Daddy was so very cautious.

Singapore was the depository for a good deal of the British wealth for the entire Far East. Most of the gold reserves were stashed away in banks there, including the one where my father was Chief Executive Officer. He had to take responsibility for his position. He and twelve other top bankers—American, French, and English—had to stick together to fight the enemies of the Empire of Japan and the Third Reich.

The bankers knew the Japanese were coming and had been told that the city was going to be surrendered that day. The bankers, twelve devoted patriots and courageous gentlemen, held a meeting and decided to destroy the currency. They would burn the paper and throw out all the silver to the coolies in the street. Anything to prevent the Japanese from winning all that money.

Daddy and his comrades knew that there was little or no hope for the victory of the Allies at this time. Therefore, they took the gold reserves and hid them in the Singapore swamps before the city fell. With discretion, and on the day Mummy and I flew away, the twelve international bankers, including U.S. citizens who had remained behind, British subjects, and other citizens at war with the Axis powers, performed this task dutifully.

That same night the Japanese intelligence service questioned Daddy and the other bankers who were not able to escape during the big crunch. They told the Japanese that the reserves had been shipped seven days previously. The twelve bankers told the same story, yet when the Japanese High Command checked with their Secret Service they were told that the gold reserves had not been shipped out since they had intercepted or destroyed most outbound ships.

The Japanese returned to my father and the other bankers and

28

asked again where the reserves were. They became angry, demanding, and finally, violent. The bankers would not tell. No one will ever know just how my father and the bankers were tortured and how they suffered, but they were faithful to their respective countries and to each other. It was a miracle of common human loyalty.

For approximately six months, my father and the bankers were tortured in grueling, prolonged agony. As exposed in the transcripts of the trial which was held in Manila for the war crimes of Field Marshall Yamashita—the infamous "Tiger of Malaya"—and his staff, the techniques were described as "barbarous."

Daddy and the bankers were shot, killed mercilessly in the spirit of the most hateful iniquity.

So, in New York, one day a special-delivery messenger arrived at our door. It was late afternoon and I was just having a spot of tea with Mummy. It was a letter from the International Red Cross, through whom Mummy was sending various parcels to Daddy in Singapore, including food, clothing, and medicine. Since the Swiss were neutral during the war, this organization acted as an intermediary for foreigners interned in enemy countries. Mummy was dependent upon Count Folk Bernadotte, a cousin of the King of Sweden and the head of the International Red Cross.

Mummy read the note quickly and entered the sitting room, clutching it in her hand. She sat down across from me at the table.

She calmly said, "Robert, I have something very important to tell you. I don't know how to express this." She was stern, holding back the slightest hint of tears. "This is the most heartbreaking event that has happened to anyone. Daddy is dead. He is no longer alive and has been sent to Heaven." She hesitated a moment. "God knows that he was murdered."

"What are you talking about?" I asked.

"Daddy will not be coming back. We have to be brave. If you want to cry, cry. But go into your room and cry alone. It is not nice to show one's feelings."

I was seven and I did not want to cry. I held the air inside my lungs and swallowed hard. I was so used to not having Daddy around that it just didn't faze me.

Well, from that point on, we had to be extra strong. There was just the two of us. Mummy had the highest hopes for me, so we would look to the future and pursue the goals that Mummy set out for us.

Years later, when my mother died, my sister Annabelle acted in a similar way.

I was serving as acting coach to Jackie Curtis, the late lamented Warhol affiliate, playwright, and poet, and I was over at his apartment on 14th Street. Annabelle rang me up.

"Come home immediately," she demanded. "Take a taxi. Something very important has happened."

"Well, what is it?" I asked expecting the worst.

"I didn't want to tell you over the telephone," she replied. "But Mummy has had a terrible hemorrhage. I don't think she's going to last very long. She's not dead yet."

"Where is she?"

"The New York Hospital," Annabelle replied.

"Can I go there now," I asked.

"Yes. Take a taxi there. Do you have money?"

"Yes, some."

"Then take a taxi and after that, come straight home. If you don't have enough money, I'll take care of it. Now go see Mummy." Annabelle hung up the phone.

I headed for the hospital. It was seven o'clock on Sunday evening, January 6, 1982. I saw Mummy lying there, helpless, an oxygen mask over her face. It was strange to see Mummy so still and it was perhaps the first time I ever saw her so vulnerable. That didn't last long. As soon as Mummy saw me, she snatched the mask off her mouth.

"Oh, it's you," she said smugly.

"Mummy, dear. How are you feeling?"

"How the hell do you think I feel? I've just had a severe cerebral hemorrhage! Can you understand me? Or is my voice slurred?"

I said, "No, your voice is as sharp as a tack. As always."

"Well," she said, "what do you look like? At least you're not in women's clothes. Praise the Lord. But I see you're wearing mascara. And you have your eyebrows painted up like a tart! But then that's you. What can I do?"

"You look all right, Mummy," I declared.

"For just having had a cerebral hemorrhage, you mean! I'm paralyzed on my right side. You say my voice is not slurred. Well, that's a miracle. You can go home now. I'm tired and I don't want to be bothered."

"I spoke to the doctor and he said your heart is very strong."

"I hope it's not that strong because I don't want to survive. If I do, then I realize, being the well-read lady that I am, that if I survive this stroke, I'll end up in the realm of senility within a matter of months, if not weeks. I'm a proud lady and I don't want to depend upon my children in my great old age that God has granted me. After all, I am over ninety. I do not want to go gaga. Besides, I no longer want to see you making a Ringling Brothers, Barnum & Bailey circus of your life anymore. I want to die with my pride intact. Now get out and leave me alone! Perhaps by the time you get home, I'll be dead. I believe in God and I want to meet my God today."

"Mummy, don't talk that way," I protested.

"Don't talk *that* way," she scolded. "Now get out! OUT! OUT! I'm tired. I'm going to rest."

That was the last I heard of Mummy. I hailed a taxi and was home a half hour later. I was there twenty minutes when the phone rang. It was the doctor from the hospital to announce the death of Lady John Hesse.

Now Mummy would be free from dealing with my shenanigans— in her own words, "the cross she had to bear."

Mrs. Christian Herter moved back into 1010 Fifth Avenue, so Mummy decided that we would stay with Granny in the tranquil surroundings of

Grammercy Park. I almost never went beyond the confines of the small, peaceful neighborhood, and when I went outdoors at all, it was to chase and grab hold of Bernadette "Bunny" Breckenridge's long red braid and pull on it. I wanted to trade the Mickey Mouse watch that Annabelle gave me on my eleventh birthday for that amazing braid.

In 1946, Mother drove the Bentley to our home in Forest Hills Gardens in Queens. We had bought the home in 1932, in the Depression, and the house had cost a fraction of what it was actually worth. Forest Hills Gardens begins at Forest Hills Inn, a once fashionable hotel. The sidewalks are made of round multicoloured stones—the streets themselves are paved with red bricks. Old gaslit lampposts line the street, fifteen and a half feet tall. Consisting of just over a hundred large Tudor houses, the neighborhood is so exclusive that they chain off the road at night. A bridge about four stories high guards the entrance at the Inn. The one and only black resident of this very Anglo-Saxon community was Dr. Ralph Bunche, winner of the Nobel Peace Prize in 1950. When he died, the house was sold to its current owner, Jimmy Breslin.

I attended Kew Forest Country Day School, a private co-ed school founded in 1915 and run by an old spinster. Each day a chauffeur drove me to school and retrieved me afterwards. The school was not as unique as St. David's, but it was a fine place to learn. Mrs. O'Dowd taught me English with great skill and Mr. Patterson taught me my favorite subject, history, in which I excelled. I delved into Mark Twain's *Huckleberry Finn* with enthusiasm. I can't remember loving a book more. Like many other pre-adolescents, I yearned to take off and be an explorer like Huck. Unlike most boys of my age, however, I was kept in confined environments and entered the world of boarding school lunacy a year later.

From as far back as I can remember, we spent our summers in Dark Harbor, Maine, where the elite mingled with the elite and indulged in the leisure activities that the pretentious Islesborough Country Club provided us with: boating, fishing, golf, horseback riding, and even tennis, which I dreaded long before it became popular.

Mummy associated there with the Auchincloss family. Jackie Onassis's mother was an Auchincloss. Louis was a society writer who had a son my age. I once spent ten days with the family on their sprawling estate, but I can't recall much of what went on. All those sporting activities kept my mind in a whirl, and memories of long-ago summers now are a blur.

ADOLESCENCE AT
PORTSMOUTH PRIORY

5

IN SEPTEMBER of 1947, the prospect of being sent off to boarding school, especially one run by the English chapter of the order of Saint Benedict, was frightening, to say the least—even if it was near Newport, Rhode Island, and a short walk from the beach. The official name of the school was The Benedictine School of St. Gregory the Great, but we called it Portsmouth Priory. A priory is the second largest community of an Order (an abbey is the largest) and is run by cloistered monks. The monks are ordained and have taken their vows in England. Some are priests and some are brothers (a brother is like a nun).

When I arrived, I was highly skeptical of going to live in a monastery with monks in robes. I thought I was going to jail. It was medieval—like going back in time to the Middle Ages. Surprisingly, however, they were very liberal. For instance, they didn't check out to see if we were going to daily Mass. This lack of insistence seemed rather odd— "Let your conscience be your guide" was their obvious motto. As we were already members of the church, they apparently decided they could be rather liberal with their standards. Actually, it was a very good psychology. The priests and brothers put their trust in us, and although I wouldn't ordinarily attend Mass every morning, I was happy to have the freedom of choice.

On the other hand, the school was similar to an English private institution—very, very fancy, and very, very regimented. Breakfast, lunch, and supper were served at a precise hour every day. The food was lousy. With the money they charged, one would think the food would surpass that of jail food quality. It was healthy, of course, but dull. It was the same damn typical English breakfast every morning: sausages, toast in racks, mush (porridge they called it—some sort of oatmeal or farina), fried kippers, bacon, eggs—and everything was cold! They had their own staff of waiters for us, not members of the clergy, but teenage boys from a nearby town. They would come in to do the domestic work. They asked, "How do you like your eggs?" and by the time the food came back, it was cold. I think it was a deliberate part of the training process.

At lunchtime, we had soup, always too hot but hearty nevertheless, and a salad; followed by two baby lamb chops, mashed potatoes, carrots and peas, all of it quite bland. Every Monday we knew what we were going to have, and so on throughout the week. Always the same menu, there was no variation and certainly no surprises.

Entertainment came by way of film, ROTC training, as well as theater. Our drama club put on amateur plays and I played all sorts of roles, both male and female. After all, it was an all-boy school. We did *Romeo and Juliet* (I played both leads on different occasions), and wrote our own plays. Parents would attend the productions, although the monks preferred to keep them away as much as possible, allowing only one visit per month. After all, it was a monastery and they wanted to keep the influence specific. Once a year we had our big production attended by all.

Dormitories consisted of four boys to a room. There were two beds in one corner and two beds in another and a door in between. I had a dresser and a foot locker in which I folded up all my clothes very neatly. There was a communal washroom in the hall (no sinks in the room—monastic style), showers, and a bathtub for boys who couldn't stand up in the shower due to polio or some sort of infantile paralysis or physical mishap. There were always a few spastic students, even in the finest of schools. In fact, I recall one boy who had one withered arm. He had no use out of it—it was a defect at birth, similar to the German Kaiser who had one arm smaller than the other. In the case of our schoolmate, his arm had been twisted in delivery and it never grew to normal size. The other arm was perfectly normal, creating a very strange sight, very dramatic indeed. His face wasn't bad looking, of Midwestern German descent.

My roommates were three boys from very wealthy families. There was Rudolph (Rudy) Wurlitzer, whose father was president of the Wurlitzer Piano Company, makers of fine pianos and also the first makers of the jukebox. They had loads of money.

Carl Busch, also of German-American stock, was of the Anheuser-Busch family, the makers of beer. His father owned a baseball team, either the St. Louis Braves or the Cardinals. Carl arrived at school in a private train with his family, displaying their overly-sophisticated pretension. The town of Portsmouth is very tiny and they made quite an impression.

Larry De Sariez, a very light Puerto Rican, occupied another bed. His family owned RinCon Rum and were the biggest landowners in Puerto Rico, and still are. His mother was from Spain and his father from Puerto Rico. They shipped her from overseas to maintain their pure Spanish blood.

Gabriel LaRosa was a roommate for a time. His family were not exactly a household word in America, but close to it. It was the name of a popular spaghetti at the time, LaRosa. I don't know if they're still in business, but it was a big name brand at the time. They had a few dollars, too.

One incident I'll never forget during my stay at Portsmouth was when the library caught on fire. They suggested that I was responsible, but could never prove it. "Someone" had rolled up little balls of newspaper and lit them by the library. The fire department informed the faculty that it was a deliberate act of vandalism. Apparently, one of the balls had not burned completely. They suspected everyone in my dormitory, in fact, and we were all sent to a psychiatrist in Providence.

"Who set the library on fire?" asked one of the monks.

"We all did," I confessed. "We were all in on that."

It wasn't a prank, but a revenge on Anselm, a brother from England who annoyed us by investing so much worry in his precious library that we'd figured we'd give him something to really worry about. We had hoped that the fact that forty percent of the books had been burnt would be somewhat disturbing to Brother Anselm.

The psychiatrist, a portly, bald-headed, pink-faced Austrian Jew by the name of Von Brock, was a disciple of Sigmund Freud. Dr. Emil Von Brock introduced us to subjects that we had never even considered at the tender age of thirteen.

"Vat do you do at dat boys' school," he asked. "It is a blatant display of homosexuality."

"I don't know what you're talking about," I protested.

"Do you know what homosexuality iss?" he persisted.

We were dumbstruck.

He attempted an explanation and further talked to us about drug addiction. He bragged that he was the foremost specialist on the subject in America.

"I never heard of it," I said. "What does that have to do with me?"

"I deal with drug addicts all over the entire Eastern seaboard."

"Why are you telling me this?" I wondered aloud.

"Because you are a pyromaniac!"

I didn't know what this meant either, and the lunatic doctor couldn't define it for me. Instead, he continued with his examination.

"Did anyone touch you? Do you masturbate together? Do you have *mutual* masturbation?" He was full of questions.

I played dumb. It was the first time I had heard these terms.

Well, the fire caused an uproar, but the grandest episode at Portsmouth Priory was when I tried to kill—no, I never tried to kill him, but—

At the tender ages of thirteen and fourteen, it is not especially unusual for boys to masturbate. Dr. Von Brock made us quite aware of this. However, while many of the boys practiced the habit publicly, I thought it should never be more than a private practice, that it wasn't quite appropriate to do it in front of others. However, in the darkness of our dormitory chambers, it was quite the thing to do at night. Meanwhile, Larry was always eager with me—I was one he wanted to share the duties with. He would bump into me, touch my ass, and provocatively play around.

Nearing the end of May one year, Larry and I were on the roof of Portsmouth Priory, a mansard roof. I was sitting on the stone ledge of the roof and Larry came and sat next to me. Suddenly, he opened his fly and pulled out a hard-on, and pulled my head onto his cock. I got very annoyed. I grabbed him behind the thighs, pulled him with all my might. He fell over my head, over the roof, and came crashing down two stories and landed in the grass. What else could I do at the time? Who was he to presume that I would participate in his charade? In effect, I taught him a divine lesson.

The headmaster, the Reverend Prior, thought something strange had been going on. We had been seen by some tattler, going up to the roof.

"What were you doing on the roof?" he asked.

I said, "Taking in the view."

Yet again, they suspected foul play. It seems Larry had landed in the grass with his fly still open. The Reverend Prior asked me what happened.

"I don't know," I said innocently. "When I descended the steps, I noticed Larry lying there in the grass."

"Did you push him?" the headmaster persisted.

"What? No! I don't know what happened. We were just going to view the ocean."

"You're not supposed to be up there," he scolded.

"Well . . ."

"Well," he commanded, "you can be dismissed."

The ambulance came and took Larry away. He, naturally, did not say a word as to what had happened.

Larry was in two casts with two broken legs from June (when he was sent home) until he came back to school in September and the casts were not removed until October.

Until my graduation from Portsmouth Priory at sixteen, I participated in sports (which I didn't particularly enjoy) such as soccer, (my only consolation was pretending that the ball was the head of somebody I didn't like as I kicked it around), boating (I made the team), tennis, and swimming.

I participated in music classes (also not my preference) and learned to play the piano.

History was my forte. I excelled in it and it was with that youthful exuberance that I pursued the subject further at Georgetown University in Washington, D.C.

THE GEORGETOWN
EXPERIENCE

6

AFTER four years in the jail known as prep school, I was off to the penitentiary of a highly established university. It was like moving from a county jail to a state prison! Run by the Society of Jesus, the Jesuits, the Georgetown faculty was certainly uptight. They were not nearly as fair as the Benedictines and far more judgmental. About 60 percent of the professors at the time were Jesuits and 40 percent were lay instructors, either married or single. Now I think there are over 80 percent non-Jesuit professors at the school. Statistics printed in a March 27, 1985, article in *The New York Times* stated that there is a rapid decline in Jesuit teachers all over the country. In 1970, there was a total of 9,000 Jesuits in the order and now there are only 6,000.

I was a bit frightened of the nation's capital when I first moved there because it was dominated by blacks. It was like walking through the streets of Harlem. I wasn't necessarily prejudiced against blacks, but I had never had any dealings with them. I was in a state of confusion—emotional chaos. Washington then was a filthy, horrible slum except, of course, for Georgetown. Begun under the Johnson Administration, the city's urban renewal efforts didn't mean much until Carter took office.

Georgetown, founded in 1789 by the Society of Jesus, whose leader was St. Ignatius Loyola, was one of the first and foremost institutions in the United States to deal with uncommon liberal subjects and matters.

For example, they had an exchange program with the all-black Howard University on the other side of town. I was exposed to black culture and was taught black history (including the history of black Catholics in America). Here I was first acclimatized to blacks, although if there were any black students at Georgetown, I didn't see them.

Georgetown was, and remains, an excellent seat of learning in this country, of the highest standards. The school of medicine is particularly outstanding.

Slowly but surely, I was becoming aware of my sexual feelings—and it wasn't women who were on my mind. I kept myself busy by visiting the numerous museums in Washington, including the Smithsonian, the National Gallery, and the Corcoran. Then I discovered some interesting hangouts, now long gone. The "High Seas," for example, a true sailor's bar (even though there was no port to speak of in Washington) became extinct after only a short time.

We were all in the closet and there were only a few places of refuge for us. When I met someone I was attracted to, I asked few questions. Rather, we would find some dingy hotel in the black section of town, such as the Cecil Hotel in Southeast D.C. Everything was hush, hush, sweet Charlotte.

Spies were all over campus, so there wasn't a chance of bringing anyone to our rooms. Heterosexual and homosexual alike, we all had to take extra precautions and depend on déclassé, extremely shoddy places. The employees of the hotels barely gave us a second glance when we walked into their establishments.

Amongst both student and faculty, there were known to be certain hours when one could walk into the men's room to get a blow job. Those who wanted to know knew the precise time and location. Lunchtime at a certain toilet in a certain building was very popular. Very much discussed by those into it, it became increasingly popular, much more than in prep school. We were all becoming oh-so-aware of sexual perversion. In the evenings, we could stroll down to the bayou, an isolated dense place of wilderness, and participate in our activities. One can hardly imagine what went on down there.

Washington was very Southern then and Southerners tend to be rather depraved. One educator in particular, a prominent professor from Howard University, was quite a renowned sexual deviate. He kept his dead mother propped up in a chaise lounge at the table, embalmed, of course, for over a month after her death. What a juicy scandal that was!

During my first year at Georgetown, the president took me into his office and said, "Put it under covers or in the shade." I looked at him dumbfounded, and he continued, "No more limp wrists for you." Obviously he had been keeping a close watch on my antics. "And don't go near Howard University," he scolded.

My mother closed her eyes to this matter. She preferred to believe that I was hanging out with the Walsh-Maclean sisters, whose great aunt was Evelyn Walsh-Maclean, the owner of the Hope Diamond. The Walsh-Macleans, along with a bevy of eligible Catholic schoolgirls, were invited to the Georgetown dances. Times have changed. Now there are gay clubs at the universities. Georgetown even has two gay associations now. At Harvard and Yale—and at every college and university—there are open organizations for homosexuals. They are totally accepted today for what was once grounds for dismissal.

MARRIAGE

7

I WAS twenty-one and greedy and Joan—the daughter of a chewing gum mogul—was three years older. I won't give her last name as I caused the lady great pain. It was 1955. I had just graduated from Georgetown. I was about to enter upon a teaching career.

I met Joan at a very chic party in the Village, on Washington Square. We soon married, and I was getting an income from her, thanks to a pre-nuptial agreement. We were married for less than a year.

I started running around with young men, and she saw me in a dress. That drove her to the bins, to the lunatic society. The poor woman was a terrible bitch. She had a complete nervous collapse—destroyed our home, smashed everything she could lay her hands on. She was very much in love with me.

I've just eliminated that episode from my mind—it's as if it didn't happen. I try not to think about it. It was so shoddy of me, so sordid. I try to forget it.

Joan is all over the world these days. Her father finally died, the clever bastard. The pre-nuptial agreement was aborted by the courts. I ended up without getting a penny and it cost me money in the end. My advice is not to marry for money. It cost me thousands in legal expenses.

I had to earn a living once more, and that started *me* on my way to a nervous breakdown.

PROFESSOR MARGO HOWARD-HOWARD

8

IT WAS during my years at Georgetown that I decided what my vocation would be: teaching. I took a job with the New York Public School System. This lasted less than a year.

They drove me crazy, those adolescents. I was teaching history at a co-ed school across the Williamsburg Bridge in Brooklyn. It was the first time I had a nervous collapse in my life.

I taught American history to third-year high-school students. Before this, I had served my time as substitute teacher for twelve months, as policy required. That same year, I was very busy working on two thesis projects that were published in book form. The first one, "Famous American Duels and Hostile Encounters," could have been the future story of my life. It was a history of duelling from the Hamilton-Burr affair until the last known duel in America at the end of the nineteenth century. "Famous American Mansions" was the story behind the construction of many great houses. They were built mostly at the request of rich men's wives. The women wanted to outdo each other in building the biggest and fanciest house.

Several thousand of these slim volumes were printed. I would not be surprised if they were still being used in classrooms around the country.

After filling in as a substitute all over the city, I was appointed to teach full-time. The area of Brooklyn was much the same as it is now: a mixture of Puerto Ricans, Hasidic Jews (who had their own Yeshivas), Poles, Ukranians, and blacks. My class of forty was half Puerto Rican, about 15 percent black, and the rest working-class whites.

The girls were worse than the boys. I tried to keep them quiet by dressing conservatively with a suit and tie and a short haircut, but they rejected me and my image, and were terrifically rude. I continued to try to teach them history. My distinction, overlooked by the school system, was to be among the first to go out of my way to teach black history.

To be in charge, one must command a certain respect and attention. I did not command the one or the other. When I turned around, they would make derogatory remarks in Spanish and nasty innuendos like "*maricón*," which is "faggot" in their native tongue. The evil little monsters made fun of me to the point of driving me into a nervous frenzy. One time one of them threw a bottle at me. It was becoming more and more terrifying. I endured nine months like this.

One of my two soul comrades at Eastern District High School was an English teacher by the name of Joseph Hussey. He, too, found working conditions very stressful and left quietly to seek a position in a private school after putting up with the public school wild animals for two years. The other was Muriel Jacobs, an older science teacher who extended her courtesy by inviting me over for supper on a couple of occasions to her home on Long Island. Both Joseph and Muriel accompanied me on countless lunches and drinking sessions. Their consolation was gratifying, but not enough.

One day I just had enough of it—my mind went. It snapped! I had a complete breakdown in the classroom. It must have been building up for a long time. I had acquired a gun in Florida during Christmas vacation. I walked into this gun shop in Fort Lauderdale. In those days, it was so easy to get one.

"May I have a gun please?"

"Certainly. What kind?"

"A thirty-two please. And a box of bullets to go with it."

It was for the grand sum of fifty dollars. Now I was a pistol-packin' mama.

I came to class with this gun in my briefcase every day. The spring term was just about over. Then one day, during an extraordinarily unbearable moment in class, I whipped out the gun and aimed at two of the students. Enough was enough! I shot one in the leg and one in the hand before they came and took me away. They dragged me into an ambulance and took me to King's County Hospital. I was then sent over to the West Hills Sanitarium. Indeed, I was the victim of a complete mental breakdown. Those kids had really gotten to me. It was one particularly rude Puerto Rican girl who was the recipient of the wound in the leg. Every time I turned around in the classroom, it was her voice that stood out as the most annoying.

The story was covered by *The Daily Mirror* and *The Brooklyn Eagle*, two unworthy papers no longer in existence. The story "Teacher Explodes" was found on page four in both journals.

The criminal charge against me was thrown out of court when the judge announced he was going to commit me. This comparatively mild sentence was due to the efforts of D. C. Murray, the F. Lee Bailey of the 1950s, who was able to have the charge of felonious assault with a deadly weapon dismissed due to the fact that I was mentally deranged.

I was declared mentally ill, stayed one day at the state hospital, and was transferred to a private institution, the West Hills Sanitarium in Riverdale, The Bronx.

Life at West Hills consisted of a day-to-day ritual to cure my unbalanced state of mind. In the mornings, shock treatments were given, followed by lunch, psychotherapy, and group therapy or afternoon relaxation periods. First thing in the morning, the nurses and doctors entered the ward and injected a dose of insulin into my shoulder. Insulin, of course, is for diabetes, and takes all the sugar out of the body. A nurse would cover me with a sheet, tie down my chest and feet, and I'd go into an insulin coma for several hours. I awoke feeling very groggy. A nurse brought me a giant cup of molasses to restore the sugar level in my body. These treatments lasted ninety days.

After lunch, if a group therapy was not planned, we would play bridge or go outside for tennis or swimming. Being a private hospital, it was very luxurious and full of extra amenities.

While I was there, D. C. Murray, criminal lawyer extraordinaire, prepared for my release. Freedom came in 1957. I moved back to Forest Hills Gardens and was placed on social security disability. Few knew of my plight. It was kept very hush-hush in those days, since any encounter with asylums or even psychiatrists was considered a disgrace! Even having cancer was shameful! It just wasn't talked about. If one had a relative in any of these situations, it was kept under wraps.

I now lived alone with my mother, and Annabelle, my sister, visited on weekends. Annabelle worked at Citicorp's new building at 399 Park Avenue. During the time I was recovering, I read often, wrote, and enjoyed the luxury of having three servants to attend me.

I was convinced that no one understood me. Unsure of my goals, I didn't know what my lifestyle should be. I was confused and confounded after having come out of nine months in the asylum. I searched for comrades in Manhattan's Greenwich Village. First it was once a week, then twice, and soon I was spending nearly every night in Manhattan. When I informed Annabelle that I intended to take a place in the city, she insisted that she find me a safe and secure apartment. I moved to a posh high-rise apartment on Central Park West complete with a cooperative doorman to whom Annabelle slipped a few dollars to watch over me and make sure I wasn't entertaining overnight guests. The pressure of being constantly looked after was quite displeasing, so I decided to seek out my own place. I found a quaint apartment on West 74th Street.

I remained quite conservative at first. I lived on West 74th Street right off Broadway. I was a bachelor, very much a loner, and doing a lot of reading. I shunned people who tried to befriend me. I wanted to be alone, like Greta Garbo. There's a certain time in your life when you want to be alone. You just want to be in your own world and you want to make it in your world.

At the same time, I was becoming intrigued with lunatics and drag queens. I was affected. Then I met Deanna Esra, "Kora Pearl" Kane, Tommy "Lana" Lavin, and other people leading the underground existence. Deanna once said to me, "Oh, you have a beautiful face. You should try on this make-up." Kora offered me a wig and Lana loaned me a dress.

I decided to give a party for my newfound friends. My hair was getting longish and cut in the new "Italian boy" look. I guess I was going against tradition. Deanna pulled me into the bathroom and began applying make-up; it lit up my face and enhanced my features. It was a lark that stuck. Most of all, I liked the way I looked.

I was living off my trust funds and Japanese compensation checks, not very much, but enough to get by. Then I entered the realm of drugs. I began with pills. I met a fellow who was attracted to me and who said, "try this" and "try that," and I tried this and I tried that and formed a habit which became increasingly expensive. I had to have drugs, and my income was no longer providing for it. Some of the other queens were hustling the streets for money, so I followed in their high-heeled footsteps. In 1957 I started using pills—anything that turned me up, down, or sideways. In 1959, I developed a moderate heroin habit and found myself on the streets more and more.

Escape was the word. The grand escape. I didn't have to worry about what most people had to worry about. There was no pressure of an everyday routine job. I did not have a family to support, no obligations, virtually no responsibilities except when, where, and how I was to get my next fix.

MUMMY'S ADVICE

9

ONCE Mummy said to me, "Bobby, I want to talk to you rather seriously. You know, I am a very well-educated woman and I understand most things in life, having been exposed to almost everything God has created in the world. I can understand or try to understand your homosexuality.

"I realize you are a homosexual and I am not too perturbed by it. To me, it's an unnatural way of life, but I can accept it and understand it, and bear the cross God has given me. I knew, in my debutante days, many young men we called 'fancy gentlemen' because they were slightly effete. However, they were honored and respected. With their educational credentials and fine background, they did something with their lives. They worked and got somewhere in the world.

"But you! I can't understand it for the life of me! If I died today, I would die uncomprehending. Why must you make a Ringling Brothers and Barnum and Bailey circus of your life by wearing those dresses? You do not look like a woman! You look like a clown!"

MY FIRST MINK

10

BETWEEN 1957 and 1964, there were four of us: Shelley, Geraldine, Barbara, and myself. Lonely men in search of sex strolled Central Park South, checking out the merchandise. The fashion vogue was long hair, tight dresses, and alluringly high-heeled shoes. Make-up was at its most pronounced: lashes caked with oodles of mascara, eyeliner streaked clear past the end of the eyelid, skinny pointed eyebrows, white and pasty pancake face powder, and glossy, sticky scarlet-red lipstick. *Au naturel* was *au revoir*. Fees were inexpensive. Twenty-five dollars for a "french," fifty dollars for a (supposed) piece of pussy, higher rates for an added depraved delight. We all had our specialties and methods for enticing the prowling gentlemen. Shelley was direct in her approach. When she saw a potential john, she would say, "Allow me to french you to get it hard." She would take him behind a bush. The man would be noticeably nervous, but would be enthralled by Shelley's overtly sexy talk and mannerisms. Shelley knelt by the man's crotch and worked him into a frenzy and he would slip her a couple of twenties. Our rule of thumb was to always work fast. After two or three hours of work, it was time to fix ourselves up and begin anew.

Wandering into the Essex House Hotel—conveniently located plus you couldn't find a more elegant *pissoir* in all of Manhattan—we were so stunning that the hotel concierges could not tell us apart from regular female patrons. Neither could the ladies' room attendant, for that matter.

One evening I strolled into the powder room, wearing an old tweed coat, my twelve-dollar thrift-shop special, and digested my fix of heroin. I headed straight for a compartment, relieved myself, rushed back out, and gazed in the mirror. I was enchanted. I was charmed. I was high on dysoxine. I sat in the fancy pink lounge, lit a cigarette, and glanced at the other powder room patrons. Just then a fat old bag appeared, looking like a wreck, surely one of the lowest forms of life. However, she did have on a ranch mink coat, which I estimated to be worth at least $10,000. I'm sitting in the lounge, thinking to myself, Look what went in the *pissoir*, baby. In other words, thinking of picking up that coat of hers as soon as she hung it on the hook. I thought, Go inside. Take the coat . . .

But she did not want to hang up her coat like the rest of the world. She took it into the stall with her, threw it over the door, and I'm looking at that mink coat and feeling a bit high.

I promptly took off my tweed coat. I stood up, placed my coat on the couch, looked again at the mink, and went up to the stall. I crossed back to the couch. I went back to the stall. I went over to that stall four times. Meanwhile, she sat there plopping away.

I said to myself, Miss Margo, if you hesitate and procrastinate, you'll get nothing—if you don't do it now, then you'll never have a mink coat in your life. And I never had one before. I went over, grabbed the mink coat, and there was a scream. It was a scream one could hear as far as 125th Street in Harlem—it sounded like murder most foul! Piercing! I dropped the mink coat on the floor. Ruth, Sylvia, Bernice, or whomever— the low-class woman, certainly no lady, tried to apprehend me. She had gotten so excited that she opened the door, her panties falling around her ankles, tripped, and fell on the floor.

I immediately picked up the coat and draped it over my shoulders.

She screamed and grunted, "Ah, help!"

As I went into the lobby, the hotel guests and bellboys were gathering around the door.

"What's going on in there, ma'am?"

I said, "Oh. Some lady is having an epileptic seizure. Excuse me."

I briskly walked about twelve or fifteen feet to the 58th Street exit.

As I spun through the revolving door, I saw a woman stepping out of a cab. I quickly slid into it.

"Downtown," I said. "Take me downtown!"

That is what I call "My Conquest." There! I had it—my first ranch mink coat wrapped luxuriously around me.

A NEAR-MISS

11

A FEW days later, I was parading my charming new garment on the grand boulevard of Broadway. Underneath I was wearing a creamy chiffon dress, ivory silk stockings, and gold pumps. A lovely Cadillac convertible, powder blue, 1951, glided by and the gentleman driving asked if I'd care for a ride. He was no more than forty-five years old, dressed in a grey and black pin-striped suit, a sure-fire corporate executive.

"Certainly. Why, thank you," I said, and stepped gracefully into the automobile.

Studying my figure and winking awkwardly, he asked me where I lived.

"I can't bring you to my place," I told him. "I'm living with a friend, a girlfriend, and she's not in the same business as I am."

It was a lovely evening. The sun was setting beneath a cerulean sky. Travelling up the West Side Highway, we decided to do our business near Grant's Tomb—where Ulysses Simpson Grant and his wife Julia Dent Grant recline in peaceful slumber. Their souls, I'm sure, have ascended to Heaven and glory.

The trick said, "If you french me, I'll give you fifty dollars."

Not bad, I thought—twenty was the going rate.

I received the fifty first (business before pleasure, as ladies of the evening will say), and I bent down to unzip the executive's fly. Unbeknownst to me or the sporting gentleman, a vice squad detective then pulled up alongside us in an unmarked car. He peered into the Cadillac, leaned out of his window, and rapped his knuckles sharply on the car window.

We were startled and tried our best to look like a couple of innocent teenagers.

"All right," he said, now standing tall and mean outside the Caddy. "Out of the car. This is a bust."

"Bust what?" I demanded.

"I've been watching you for several days, girlie, on Broadway," he said.

"How dare you," I said.

"Never mind that dare shit," he said. "You're under arrest."

He reached in to grab my hands and apply those nasty handcuffs. I shoved him, threw open the car door, and began to run. The executive in his powder blue Cadillac sped off. I ran across Riverside Drive down along 123rd Street and across to what was then the location of the Julliard School of Music. I ran along 123rd Street for what seemed like miles, in such a state of panic that I was barely looking to see where I was going. Suddenly, a red car darted around the corner and struck me down. One high heel broke. The next thing I knew I was waking up to the sound of a police siren. The police car came to a screeching halt just before my prostrate body. I opened my eyes slowly to see the same detective leaning over me.

"All right, get up. You're under arrest."

I screamed that I was pregnant and hit by a car. He gingerly helped me to my feet and guided me to the curb. The detective then escorted me to the Knickerbocker Hospital on 126th Street and Amsterdam Avenue, an institution no longer in existence. Along the way, he kept glancing at me to make sure I was all right. I faced the other way, to keep from bursting into laughter.

At the hospital, they put me on a stretcher. I screamed, "Don't touch me! Don't touch me!" Someone asked if I was pregnant. I told them I wasn't. Then a doctor came and said, "They said you're pregnant." I said I wasn't, but that my arm was broken. I had dislocated my arm in the fall, and was actually quite uncomfortable.

They put my arm back in place, put it in a sling, and then a nurse told me that I had to be examined by the doctor—a good-looking young intern, assisted by a cold, hard mannish bitch of a nurse. The nurse said that I needed a complete physical. Some drunk there said, "Yeah, give *it* a complete physical." And I said to myself, "Margo, the jig is up."

A city patrolman had been assigned to guard me—I guess the vice cop was off phoning headquarters. I knew I was going to jail unless I did something, and fast. As I was being taken down the corridor, I looked out a big window and saw the ambulance driveway about a story and a half down. I spotted a water cooler and became quite fem, all soft and limp and dainty. I said to the young patrolman, "Oh, please, officer, may I get a drink of water? I'm dying of thirst."

He said yes—and I walked over to the fountain, assessed the gains and risks one last time, quickly backed up a few steps, covered my face with my arms, took a running leap and smashed through the window. I landed on my feet, and I remember noticing I broke the heel of my other shoe. I was about in the middle of the driveway, approximately forty feet from either end of the drive. I didn't know what to do. I knew that if I tried to run either way I would be apprehended. There in front of me were several large trash cans filled with hospital refuse, so I climbed into one and covered myself with that horror. I heard the patter of flat feet, and then someone said, "She isn't in the driveway. Search the building—she must have gotten back inside."

I remained there for hours until finally the garbagemen arrived to cart off the trash. I felt the barrel tremble as it was being lifted, and screamed, "Stop! Wait!" They were just about to dump me into the machinery that compacts trash. Much to the amazement of the sanitation engineers, out of the schlock popped my head. "Well," I said, "where are your manners? Help this lady out of the receptacle." I got out and away, none the worse for wear.

THE CORK CLUB

12

FROM 1950 through 1960, there were two "in" spots for us queens, dark curious establishments where the hush-hush talk of homosexual haunting grounds could be heard. Lana was one of the most striking queens to hang out at the Cork Club, a raunchy little joint in a respectable part of town, located at West 72nd Street and Broadway. Here was the haven for the loud "Brooklyn queens" as they were called, the drags with the wildest hairdos, the crazy-colored hair, the big mouths, and the flashy outfits. It was like Berlin in the 1920s. Everything you could think of went on in those clubs: dancing with anonymous partners, shots of dope in the toilet, and curious observers taking it all in. Deanna and Lana and I would often stop at the Cork Club for a drink, for a rest, or for a quick fix. Another frequent customer was a foxy little specimen by the name of James Dean. Deanna spotted him most often and remarked to me, "Amazing how that young man just sits there, terribly attractive, and never fraternizes with anyone."

JIMMY DEAN AND ME

13

I MET James Dean in the summer of 1953, when I was on vacation from college. He was a sight to behold.

One fine day I was crusing Central Park West between 70th and 79th Streets, amongst all the other homophiles, speeding on goofballs (a combination of Seconal and Tuinal), and I caught sight of a gorgeous sandy-haired young man strolling along, hands in his pockets.

James Dean was just about coming into his own at that time. He was going to Actors Studio, and he had played a small part on Broadway and had been pointed out in the press as a great new talent. I had seen his picture in the paper, so when I saw this guy coming toward me I knew right off exactly who he was.

I said, "Hello. You're James Dean, you're a star." He smiled and said, "Are you in show business?" "No," I replied, "I go to school at Georgetown U."

He was very impressed that I recognized him. He looked at me, intrigued. My hair was crimson and cut short. I was in tight jeans and sandals. I introduced myself, and we got to talking. We had a drink in a watering hole nearby, an Irish bar of the kind that's rare in New York these days, and he invited me up to his place as it was just around the corner.

The neighborhood was then very seedy—lots of Puerto Ricans, old rooming houses, and similar horrors—but I followed him to his tiny room on the top floor of a brownstone, a little garret really, on 68th Street off

Central Park West. The place was a mess—I noticed a guitar, bongos, an incredible number of books, records, and a display of white ceramic masks on the wall. It had no windows, only a small skylight. He must have paid about eight dollars a week in rent.

He told me he had a Hollywood screen test coming up, but I didn't believe him. We all had Hollywood screen tests coming up. I told him I had a part in a TV program that was up for an Emmy nomination.

He was rather strange, a disappointment to me. He was so bad—not a hair out of place and all that stuff. You can imagine—him preening in front of his mirrors in that tiny room. Oh God, I thought, this one is even nellier than I am. Very depressing. So I sort of turned off, and got out of there as soon as I could.

I never saw him again. When I saw him, he wasn't famous, he was on the rise. But he was mentioned in the press every now and then as a new sensation. Watch for James Dean. He's going to be very big.

One day, a few years later, I was strolling down 57th Street and checked out the Playhouse marquee. In huge letters was REBEL WITH-OUT A CAUSE STARRING JAMES DEAN. My friend Deanna and I went to see it, and sure enough, it was the same James Dean whose garret I'd been invited to.

I don't need to be a star. I'm content with my own life, even with my shoulders crushed. I'm not heroic, I'm stoic.

THE BALLEY

14

THE BALLEY was a different kind of club. Nearly pitch-black and further up on the West Side, the Balley not only allowed but encouraged all sorts of activities which were then illegal. Homosexual dancing back then was considered highly immoral, but at the Balley it was "Bring on the dancing boys!" If the cops were thought to be coming, the doorman simply pressed a button which automatically turned all the lights on and everyone immediately stopped dancing.

Lana frequented the Balley more than any other queen I knew. The luck that Lana talked about often was at its luckiest at the Balley. She met one particular gentleman who bought her an entire new wardrobe, spent loads of dough on wild parties where liquor flowed like a waterfall, and even sent her to beauty school so that she could fulfill her true dream career. Unfortunately, Lana and the rest of us were so occupied with the parties, staying up for days on end, that she flunked out of beauty school. No matter, Lana was so extraordinary looking that she was able to find various supporters throughout the years. Her obsession with Lana Turner was understandable, as she really did resemble the movie star. Lana loved to tell the story of how it was actually the Top Hat Malt Shop where Lana Turner was discovered, and not the legendary Schwab's, as most people believe. She could also recite passages from various Turner movies—*The Prodigal* was her favorite and Lana named her cat "Samara" after Turner's role. Then she found out that her cat was a male, which gave the correct ironic twist to the naming. Beautiful women fascinated all of us, and the drags simply fulfilled our fantasies: We were in search of the same beauty. So what if it was we ourselves whom we chose to represent it?

It had been Lana that I was tracking down when I first met the woman with whom I would share my startling adventures. A very pretty and trim lady with straight brown hair and bangs was waiting for Lana when I approached.

"You tell that Neal Mora that I have warrants out for his arrest! You are affiliated with him!" I yelled.

The lady calmly replied in her peculiar British accent, "Don't be silly. That's between you and Mora. I have nothing to do with it. I know nothing about it."

"You're British!" I was quite enthusiastic and immediately struck up a conversation with her. She began to tell me about her recent trip to London and I told her that I came to see Lana because she owed me quite a sum of money. Deanna was there for the same reason. She further proclaimed that she had heard of me and wanted to meet, as she put it, "the legend of the West Side," but had been playing it cool. By the time Lana came along, Deanna Esra and I were pals.

"If I let you in, you better not start anything . . ." Lana was wired and her hair was full of peroxide, leaving it a shocking white.

Lana's apartment was a center of the drug trade. Dexadrine sold at the unbelievable price of ten for a dollar on the black market. It was no wonder that we had enough to get high for days. Deanna was the only one of us too sensible to take all the drugs. She'd witness our indulgences and look out for the over-indulgers. I can recall staying up for four or five days straight, making money, sleeping for twenty-four hours, and jumping back in action again! It was uncanny how debauched we could get and then just pop right back. I remember occasionally loud, murderous arguments and the ripping of dresses when things got too extreme. We were high in excess on Tuinals, which could make one quite evil. There was a sort of rivalry to see who could outdo whom in drug excess and frolic.

This isn't to say that crimes weren't committed, but for the most part, the crimes were on us! One rather warm day, Deanna was over at my apartment on 71st Street. We had the door a bit ajar to let in a nice breeze. Suddenly, a man resembling an ape and, I might add, certainly not a gentleman, appeared at the door. We were high as a kite, having taken a mixture of heroin and amphetamine—a speedball, as it was called. The man lunged for the television and demanded that we take off all our clothes. We saw the flash of a butcher knife and obeyed.

I was ferocious. I said, "Do you want to see an unnatural act?"

He stuttered when he saw the demented grin on my face and fumbled for something to say while attempting to lift the extremely heavy TV set off the floor.

Suddenly, the speed hit me and I took umbrage. I felt like a Superman (or Superwoman)! "You're not taking anything from here!" I said. I was in a rage. "This is my house! This is my friend! You're not getting nothing here!"

The sight of a maniacal nude drag queen was, apparently, too much for him to handle. He dropped the knife; I grabbed it and poked at him as he scurried out of there. Deanna fell back on the couch and put her hand on her heart. "My hero," she sang. Then it was back to work.

Deanna and I were a good team because hanging out with a real lady was good for me as it offset the fact I was truly a man. It was good for Deanna because I had a tougher approach and could get the higher prices for our services. If a trick tried to get too intimate with me, thinking I was a woman, then Deanna would throw herself on him and take care of business. Sometimes, of course, the trick preferred a queen and then it was up to me to satisfy him. We always shared our income and looked out for each other, even when times were quite rough.

One chilly October night, Deanna and I were cruising for tricks. We were dressed in our most attractive attire. Deanna was recovering from alcohol abuse and decided that she needed a drink badly. We were en route to the local bar when we passed St. Thomas Episcopal Church. I said to Deanna, "Let's go in and pray for luck." She scoffed at the idea, yet I insisted and we entered the church. I proclaimed in a loud, strident voice: "Please, God, send us two men to rob and trick before the night is over."

Deanna was mortified and slunk out of the church. I followed after her as various heads spun around to check out the ballsy drag queen. As we turned the corner, we came face-to-face with two men. They were handsome and hungry for love and proceeded to take us to the Astor Bar. I drank sixteen brandies. Deanna was so infatuated with one of the men that she no longer felt the urge for a drink. I made fifty dollars that night and Deanna met her future husband. I still contend that Deanna owes her marriage and serene retirement to my prayers.

COPS AND ME

15

I HAVE this to my distinction: I have never been arrested on the street for looking like a supposed man in women's clothes. No detective has ever stopped me and said, "What is your name? Where are you going? Are you a man or a woman?"

I was, however, arrested for soliciting, or, in other words, prostitution, as a woman.

I was taken down to the East 51st Street stationhouse and the matron searched the girls.

"I have something to tell you," I said. "I am not a woman."

She said, "I know. All you lezzies say the same thing."

I then had to produce the personal parts of my body to show her that I was truly not a woman.

I was sent to court to face, luckily, a very kind judge by the name of Randall J. Creel. He said I was mentally ill and needed a head examination to see what was wrong with me—why I thought I was a woman.

As a result, I was sent to Bellevue for thirty days' observation, sent back to court and declared sane, and sentenced to thirty days—time served.

Deanna was accused of female impersonation once. She kept denying it, baring her breasts, yet they booked Deanne and me for prostitution. We had just come from an old demented trick who was a pill addict. I had stolen all his pills, at least sixty blue devils or Tuinals. We began raving and ranting with glee. Just then a cop came along. "This is better than a Broadway show," he said sarcastically. Being high and angry and under the influence of barbituates, Deanna responded strongly.

"I'll give you a show, you motherfucker!" she said. She proceeded to throw a burning-hot cup of coffee at him. His shoulder was on fire. He flew into a rage.

I knew we were in deep trouble now. I took the remainder of the pills, around thirty, and swallowed all of them to avoid being charged with possession. I fell against the wall, slowly sliding down it like in a Marx Brothers comedy. Meanwhile, Deanna was screaming, "She's having a fit! She's prone to these fits all the time. Call Bellevue or she may die! Hurry!"

The cop had no choice. He called for an ambulance. Deanna ran to fetch help.

The next thing I recall is the scene at the hospital. Apparently I was in a coma for days, vomiting internally into my lungs, whereupon pneumonia set in. Deanna recalls my sister and my mother in deep agony as my chances for survival seemed slim. Burial arrangements were discussed. Deanna informed me that our crazy cohorts were sadly discussing who would inherit which of my costumes. At night, they lit candles and prayed for me. They began collecting money for the most extraordinary service the underground world had ever seen.

My room was filled with huge floral bouquets. My sisters, who had not spoken to me in years, had heard that this might be their last chance to show any regard for me whatsoever. The bouquets flourished. The days went on. The priest was coming in daily, giving me last rites. It all must have contributed to my survival, because I did not die at that tender young age of twenty-nine.

One day I suddenly awoke to the sight of the priest concluding the prayers for my soul. "What the hell are you doing?" I snarled. "This actress is not ready to die!" I then greeted my mother and sister.

I had been entertaining a trick at the Waldorf-Astoria. He got so excited that he became violent and bit me on the tongue. Though it was an accident, I was horrified at the blood that had splurted all over my white linen dress. I grabbed a lamp and smacked him over the head.

The cops arrived as I made my way down to the lobby. My client was sent to the hospital. He chose to press charges and I, in turn, was sent to jail on a charge of felonious assault.

I knew that if I went before the judge I'd be convicted and given a long sentence because I was a notorious drag queen prostitute by this time. So in the jail cell I melted two Hershey bars together over the toilet and covered over the entire rim.

When a guard walked by, I dipped my finger in it and sucked it very loudly. The startled guard stopped dead in his tracks. "Hey, you!" he shouted. "What is that on the toilet?"

"Shit," I replied, licking my fingers.

He immediately screamed, "Call Bellevue! Margo has flipped!"

They promptly did so and I was sent back to Bellevue. After ten days, I was released.

I don't think a day went by without some sort of bizarre experience or adventure involving myself and any number of assorted acquaintances. There were some especially intriguing characters who come to mind.

Tommy introduced me to Bill Jackson, better known as the "Hair Freak." He was a fifty-five-year-old man who liked to comb your hair to the left side and give you a hundred dollars. He had this comb which had belonged to his mother—a Spanish mantilla comb made out of tortoise-shell. He dropped by every Friday at our place on 74th Street. He was in awe of drag queens with long hair. First thing he'd do upon his arrival was wash and set my hair. Lana was very close to Jackson.

In the late fifties's, he used to pick up young boys, buy them complete outfits, wash their hair in Drene shampoo, and take them out as his daughters. In fact, Lana was once taken out that way to the St. Moritz.

Eventually, we found out that he was the vice president of a renowned publishing firm and a certified family member. I wonder if his kinsfolk knew how "Bill Jackson" transformed all those young boys.

At the same time, I was specializing in my own brand of metamorphosis. I was acting as the grand dame and trainer of young novice graduate boys into pros. I had quite an outstanding reputation and many young hustlers were interested in my approach. I trained a beautiful young drag queen named Barbara (Bobbi) to hustle the streets. We cruised the Waldorf Towers for an initial introduction. A nice Jewish man approached us and told us he wanted a ménage à trois. "Very well," I said, "but you must play by the rules. Money first."

One hundred dollars was exchanged. He brought us up to his suite and cautioned, "No noise in the apartment."

On entering, I screamed at the top of my lungs, "Pimp! Importuner of young girls!"

He was so distracted that he bribed me with two hundred dollars to leave with a terrified Barbara.

Another time we were out by the Lexington Avenue Hotel. It's suicide to hustle there because there's always police, but I was putting Barbara to the ultimate test. Barbara picked up a trick very quickly and I remained waiting downstairs in the lobby. A bit bored, I popped a few pills. The house cops became suspicious and asked me what I was doing there. Now high, I got very indignant and told them I was waiting for a friend. At that point, Barbara sauntered out of the elevator, having just turned a trick. We were both busted and taken to the station.

At the precinct house, they refused to believe that Barbara was a man. They actually took Barbara to the ladies' division. When he turned to the matron to inform her that he was really a man, she said, "We're all men in here, honey."

"But I'm a *real* man," he protested. "I don't belong here."

After some investigative research, they finally believed him. Poor Barbara was sent to Riker's for ninety days. As for me, they could not prove anything and I was released the next day.

I felt terribly guilty about this. I felt like a mother to Bobbi and it was I who had trained him. He was fascinated by us and latched onto our lifestyle. He really bought the scene, but I don't think he ever forgave me for letting him get into that risky situation. When he was released I let him stay at my apartment. I nodded out and the next thing I knew my handbag was gone along with $685. Even though he was born on my birthday, that was inexcusable. I had just stolen that money myself from a

INDEX OF PHOTOGRAPHS

john that evening, along with Gloria Bradley, who had the distinction of being the ugliest hustler around.

Gloria Bradley was a hairy, disgusting woman with a huge belly and false teeth, who used to dress in a cotton housedress, rubber thongs, hair in rollers, and a cigarette dangling out of her mouth. She had to keep a bar of soap between her legs to cover up a particularly bad genital odor. She also wore the finest perfumes, but all the perfumes in Araby couldn't wipe out her stench.

She used to say, "I don't need make-up. I'm natural." She got a lot of tricks that way. Although she had been married and had three daughters, she had a black lesbian lover named Grumpy. They had met when Gloria was an attendant at the Central Islip State Hospital. Grumpy's brother, Percy, had landed her in there when she tried to stab him. Gloria and Grumpy fell in love and became roommate lesbian lovers and bred toy poodles. One was named Pavala, or Pavvy. Grumpy, who used to curl my hair over a hot stove with a curling iron, was always high on terpin hydrate, a 35 percent codeine cough syrup which was so strong that she had to sign for it at the pharmacy.

The most beautiful queen in town was Amber, breathtakingly gorgeous and sometimes sweet. Sometimes she was about as sweet as cyanide. If Tommy Lavin was a copy of Lana Turner, Amber was a replica of Marilyn Monroe. Amber, whose real name was Tony LaRusso, took her name from the Linda Darnell film "Forever Amber" and won the prize at Jack Silverman's International Nightclub for her impersonation of Marilyn. Another exceptional drag queen was a Puerto Rican with fantastic long legs called Josephine Baker. As a boy, he looked quite butch and one would never expect he would don the female sex so well. Johnny looked like Jayne Mansfield and was the most dramatic of us queens with that great fake chest of his. We all hung out at the same West Side establishments and nowhere else could boast of such a splendid array of drag queens.

After the heyday of the Cork Club and the Balley, we all moved downtown.

Our most popular hangout was the #7. As Deanna will attest, we opened that place and closed it. Raving alcoholics, some of them straight out of the detox ward, were the habitual customers. At twenty-five cents a glass, wine, usually a dark port or muscatel, was the most popular item with whiskey at thirty-five cents for the big spenders. Therefore, if you had a drinking habit, you would drink twice as much in there. On Christmas and Easter, I would make it my goodwill mission to buy everyone in the place a bottle. The anxiety and lunacy that went on were amazing. It attracted observers who would slum around checking out the drag queens, the drug fiends, and the crazy prostitutes.

Deanna and I met and befriended Adrienne there, one of the first black drag queens in New York, who began dressing up in the 1940s when it was common to be arrested just for being gay. The cops had picked her up many times for cruising and had sent her to what is now The Jefferson Market Library to await trial. Next they were sent to Center Street where the homosexuals were segregated and confined to Riker's Island. There they worked on a farm, gave shows with make-up, and played bridge. Adrienne refers to this time as her "rest period." It was not a big deal to be arrested, after all, and after she was released, she could always get work in restaurants or doing domestic work. Rent was low—only three dollars a night for a room. Adrienne chose not to use excessive make-up and managed to look like an ordinary black woman in drag. Her hustling life was extra tough, especially when she worked in Chicago. In 1960, she was back in New York, frequenting the #7, which was open to everyone: blacks, whites, foreigners, every religious persuasion, and every criminal on the sidewalk. Owned by an ex-cop who encouraged fights, the #7 was the kind of bar you'd expect to find on a waterfront.

Diane Arbus sought both comfort and inspiration here. Amongst the lunatics, she probably felt a bit more secure with her comparably normal life, and it was a haven for some of her most fabulous subject matter for photographs. Here Diane met Patricia Morgan, who later became "Man in Rollers" to the rest of the world. Patricia, born Henry Glockovitch, was six-foot-four, built like a fullback, with a face like Jack Palance. A clever entrepreneur, he ran a limousine service with prostitutes behind the wheels of pink Cadillacs. He called it "Playboy," but had to change the name to "Bunny" when *Playboy* threatened a lawsuit. Arbus photographed Patricia with Deanna in flagellation garb.

Patricia was once picked up by a Chinese gentleman who refused to pay first. Patricia raised a ruckus, took a hammer, and beat him over the head. The neighbors heard the screaming, of course, and called the police. The Chinese man was in a coma for weeks, Patricia was sent to Elmira State Reformatory for five years, served that sentence, and was out on the streets again. He began saving his profit for hormone and silicone injections, split to Los Angeles, where his best friend, Geraldine, had gone, and changed into a woman—"corrective surgery," as it was called. Back in New York, we all agreed that she looked great with her enormous breasts and slim figure. Deanna had her daughter by then and Patricia offered to adopt it. She claimed she would give the child everything— money, education, and luxury living—with her newfound profitable project, two rooming houses in Hoboken. We all figured that Patricia desperately wanted to feel more feminine and having a daughter would do just that. As it turns out, Deanna raised her daughter magnificently, with love and honesty and an open mind.

As Deanna was settled, I became closer to Kora, who introduced me to yet another selection of characters, mostly real women. He knew the "Queen of Crime," Madame Fagan, legendary for recruiting teenage boys to burglarize houses. She was a tough old Italian hooker who had married a trick and murdered him. She had left his body in their apartment and gone down to have breakfast at an all-night cafeteria. The body was discovered immediately and the police came to arrest her for the murder. She said, "Well, I'm not leaving until I finish my ham and eggs."

Kora and I knew a painter named David, who lived with his eccentric mother in back of Yankee Stadium. She claimed to have met Marilyn Monroe while working at Payne-Whitney and displayed one of Marilyn's bras on the wall as a strange souvenir.

Kora was my close comrade, so when he fell into the first stages of severe depression, I noticed it right away. I suggested he come with me to Coney Island to visit a Dr. Whitman. We were in for a surprise. When we arrived in full make-up and dress, the doctor told Kora that since he looked so much like a woman, he ought to become a woman. The hormone treatments calmed Kora down, but much to Kora's chagrin, he began to develop small breasts. He did not want them, yet the Premarin and Provera injections were a relief to his nerves.

Dr. Whitman was quite a charlatan. In the waiting room were church pews. We often joked that we could pray all day, waiting for the doctor to treat us. His black nurse, Octavia Bush, looked more like a man than any drag queen in New York. While Waldman accepted any kind of Medicaid or insurance plan known to mankind, he would charge top dollar to the state and insist upon an extra ten dollars from each of us every time we visited. We stopped patronizing him and switched to Dr. Benjamin of Park Avenue. If Joe Lewis, champion fighter, had walked in for a routine examination, Benjamin would have told him he ought to be a woman. In would walk beautiful male specimens with bulging muscles and it was the same remark. On an early morning talk show Kora had seen him explain to the audience that before a sex operation is performed, he carefully analyzes the patient, utilizing a staff of shrinks. Dr. Benjamin was a liar, a charlatan, and a thief—and a disgrace to the Hippocratic oath.

Kora was also involved in a reckless encounter with Albert DeSalvo, better known as the Boston Strangler. He met Albert when forced to leave New York because of a warrant that was out for his arrest. Kora fled to Boston and continued his hustling career. He was tricking in a bar when Albert nudged Kora to get rid of the john he was with and go with him. Kora saw Albert on and off for three years, during which time Albert was murdering people by strangulation. Kora, who found Albert sweet and generous, had no idea that this was going on. When DeSalvo was finally apprehended and sent off to Atwater Hospital, he met his death. "The Boston Strangler" was stabbed and smothered by outraged inmates. Kora was shocked into becoming plain old Joey from then on.

SAUL HITE, THE MAN WITH THE WOODEN LEG

16

I MET "Saul Hite" in the Village, in 1959. He was an English Jewish gentleman but he was fine, very grand. I met him through a friend of mine named Jay Colby. He was an old fool who liked young boys and young drag queens and was pretty generous. He had a wooden leg. I was coming from his house one night when I met Truman Capote.

I met Saul at Jay Colby's house on West 4th Street, right around the corner from the old Riviera Bar. So I went to his apartment. He was living at 750 Park Avenue. I saw him for eight or ten months. I would go to see him once a week. He was generous in return for a little hanky-panky. He adored me, you know. He was a widower. One time, oh I was so terrible, I was taking amphetamines at the time too, one time I went to visit him in his office on Madison in the Seventies, where he worked at Sotheby's. I was high. He patted me on the cheek and I said, "What are you doing smacking me?" and he said, "No, no, it's affection." He had a cane and I took his cane—he had all this jade and porcelain on glass shelves in his office—and I smashed them all, tens of thousands of dollars' worth of rare jade. He loved it. He liked humiliation.

Then he took me one time to lunch at Soule's Le Pavilion, which was a very posh French restaurant in the Ritz Hotel on 57th Street at Park

Avenue, the Ritz Tower. I was wearing a gold linen suit. I had platinum blond hair done in a French twist, and little white cotton gloves, and who was sitting there but the Duke of Windsor. I was taking a pill that turned me into a monster. Tuinal, a very strong barbituate. It turned me evil and nasty. Saul said, "Oh, get up, it's the Duke of Windsor." So I took another pill. He said, "Sir, I'd like you to meet Margo Howard." He told me, "Sit up." I said, "How do you do, your royal highness." He said, "Oh, just fine." And Saul said, "And this is Her Grace, the Duchess of Windsor." She looked at me and made a face, and I said, "What the hell are you making a face at me for, you bulldog-faced bitch?" She made believe I wasn't there, and said, "As I was saying, David," and I said, "You heard me, you rotten bitch." And Henri Soule said, "Get out of here! How dare you!" And I said, "I'm not going anywhere." They had to drag me out.

Saul Hite stood there with his mouth hanging open. He called me up later and he said, "How are you feeling? Are you better? You were upset at lunch. I'm sorry you were upset. I shouldn't have brought you over. I thought you would be thrilled to meet them. She didn't say anything; why were you so rude? But let's not talk about that. I hope you're feeling better."

I was a monster to Saul Hite but he was a mental masochist and he enjoyed it. Once at his Park Avenue apartment I got angry with him when I told him to give me a thousand dollars and he said he had no cash, he had only fifty in cash. I said, "Well, I want more money." He said, "I don't want to give it to you because you've had enough of your substances. That amount of money will kill you."

I said, "You rotten bastard," and I took his wooden leg, which was off at the time, opened the French doors of the balcony, and threw it off from the tenth floor. It ripped through the canopy. A young woman was going by and it hit her. It hit her leg, and she had a fracture. Of course it cost tens of thousands of dollars to settle out of court.

He forgave that. He forgave everything—throwing drinks in his face, throwing coffee at him in restaurants. One gets what one's hand calls for. One day—and this was the biggest shock of my life—I had to perform the act, you know, lie down in the bed. To be graphic, he had his penis

80

up my ass. He was having a great time and all of a sudden he went, "Ahhhh." And I said, "Hurry up, will you, godammit, I have to go uptown to buy something." He went, "Uh." I said, "Are you done?" and I pushed him over and he fell on the floor and he was blue. I knew right away he was dead.

I was confounded. I said, "Oh, what am I going to do?" I got on the phone and called the doorman. I said, "Hellooo, this is Apartment ten-A, my uncle, Mr. Hite, has had a coronary or a heart attack or something. I think he's dead. Do you have a physician living in the building? Could you send somebody? I don't know what to do." He said, "Very well, just hang up." And a few minutes later—I had put a bathrobe on—a physician who lived in the building came in. He said to me, "Why don't you make yourself decent? He's had a coronary."

Saul's face had a look of religious ecstasy. I thought, oh my God, my asshole was so good that it was murderous. So the police came, but everything was all right. They knew I was a man. I put corduroy slacks on and pinned my hair up. I didn't tell them what we were doing.

He had promised to leave me all his money, but he left me nothing. He lied too. His children got it all. I did feel that it was my duty to take a few *objets d'art* when I left, a few things, a few pieces of Georgian silver, a few things like that. Chinese porcelain and jade statues. I sold some of them in antique shops on Third Avenue, but I still have quite a lot. Young Chen Dynasty porcelain. Jade statues. A Ming Dynasty horse.

THE RUSSIAN LADY

17

Nineteen fifty-nine was the year our beloved President Eisenhower was in office. The fun-loving fifties were just about over, and they looked like they were going to end with a whimper. It was a period of refined contentment, and crimes tended to be of a small nature. Even the cops were a bit bored and were trying to think of some clever ways to prevent the muggings and rapings of posh women on the Upper West Side. Operation Decoy was in effect; the cops were dressing in women's clothes to trap the bad guys. Good for the women on the Upper West Side, but not so good for us drag queens out trying to make a buck.

I had been selling my wares on Central Park South, looking out for my clients and nervously checking out the other queens to see if they were not maybe cops in disguise. It was grueling work. I decided to take a break. The all-night Rudley's restaurant on 78th Street and Broadway was close. I stepped in for a cup of coffee and a crust of bread. I was rather hungry after this hard night of pounding the pavements to get adventurous gentlemen to buy my bogus genitalia. Giving them lips, hips, and fingertips instead of the real thing.

A fragile, little old woman barged in with a big shopping bag, looked at me, and said in a heavy Russian accent, "Miss/Mr./Mrs . . . ?"

I turned to her and said, "Yes?"

She was as old as water. "May I sit with you?"

"Well," I said, looking around the place, "there are plenty of other booths and seats, but if you want to sit with me, it's quite all right, madam."

She studied me and said, "I know who you are."

I leaned close to her. "Sshhh. If you do, please don't tell anyone."

She said, "You are a police woman/man." She paused. "I have something for you." She handed me a bill.

I presumed it was a one-dollar bill and began to put it away. I said, "Thank you," but before I put it in my purse, I glanced at it. It was a hundred-dollar bill! I thought, My God! What is this woman giving me a hundred dollars for? She's as old as the hills, at least eighty, and perhaps wants me to do something freakish. An old fag-hag freak!

I said, "Ma'am, madam, do you realize what the bill you gave me was?"

"Don't worry. You'll earn it."

My God, I thought, she wants something freakish!

Meanwhile, I was starving. I yelled for Connie, the middle-aged drunk blonde waitress. "Connie, come here please!"

Connie liked stimulants, barbituates, and young boys—Puerto Ricans especially. She was a decent woman.

Nina said, "Give this lady/man/woman whatever she wants. I'll pay. Chopped steak—no hamburger! Chopped steak for her!"

Connie said, "We don't have chopped steak. Only hamburger."

Nina said, "Don't you have something nice? She's a good woman/man/lady."

This one's a lunatic, I thought, but I didn't know. Perhaps she was just trying to attract me. You never know.

She said, "You will help me, won't you?"

"That depends," I said. "What kind of help do you want?"

"I am being persecuted by the Bolsheviki."

"The Bolsheviki?"

"The Bolsheviki." Then she started speaking in Russian to me.

"I don't speak that language," I told her.

"Oh, you don't? I forgot so soon."

"So soon?"

"You will help," she pleaded. "Won't you?"

"Very well," I replied.

"Start now," she said.

My hamburger came, but Nina paid no mind. "Stop them now! We must go and save her."

She grabbed me by the arm, not even bothering to pay the check as we rushed out of Rudley's. She escorted me from 78th Street to 79th Street, cars honking as we stampeded in front of them, down the hill from Broadway to West End Avenue and on to Riverside Drive, through the park to the yacht basin via the staircase that leads to the rotunda by the water. When we reached the promenade, Nina opened her bag and pulled out a clothesline.

"Open the rope," she said.

She was insistent, so I obeyed.

"Throw the rope to her!"

I said, "Throw the rope to who?"

She looked at me like I was mad. "Are you crazy?"

"Crazy? Me? Why?"

"Can't you see Vanya out there in the water?"

"Well, I haven't got my spectacles on. Wait." I proceeded to pull my glasses out of my purse.

"Hurry," she shouted. "Please, fool, hurry!"

"Oh yes! I see her now."

"Throw the rope!"

I took the clothesline and threw it in the water.

She calmed down a bit and said something in Russian. She was waving.

"Why are you waving?" I asked.

"You did very good job. You got her out of the water. And now she's able to fly."

"Fly?"

"Can't you see? Are you blind or crazy? She is flying. Her wings were affected by water and you got her out of the water. Very good. I give you nice bonus for this."

"Where is she flying to?" I inquired.

"What is the matter with you? Can't you see? She's flying uptown towards George Washington Bridge."

"I can't see the George Washington Bridge," I told her.

"It's there! She's flying to George Washington Bridge."

"Well, I see."

"You are very good police woman/man."

"Thank you," I replied.

I had no make-up on. My hair was very long, shoulder-length, and was tied into a French twist. I had a large white knit sweater on. I did look very much like a woman.

"We go back to restaurant," she said. "I'm sure your dinner is cold. We buy you another one."

"All right," I agreed.

We got back and the waitress said she'd put the food back on the flame for us.

"No! No!" Nina protested. "Throw away! We want fresh." She turned to me. "What is your name? My name is Nina Sournin Petty. I have house around corner, private home, where my late husband and I have home in New York."

"Oh, I see."

"You know Isnoskov."

"Who?"

"Komissar Isnoskov of NKVD."

"NKVD?"

"He is still trying to murder me since 1917."

"Really?"

"I need your help. You are a big strong woman/man."

"Why do you call me woman/man?"

"Never mind that. I had a brother who liked to dress as a ballet dancer, in women's clothes, too."

"Oooohhh."

"I will pay you a hundred dollars every day to protect me."

I was at this time hustling and dabbling in heroin. Money did not come that easy. After all, one hundred dollars was two tricks, sometimes four.

86

"Where do you live?" she asked.

"I live at 142 West 74th Street."

"You have house there?"

"I live in a rooming house."

"Why do you live in furnished room? I have full house for you."

"Well . . ."

"Please come," she interrupted. "We have champagne."

She took me around the corner and up the stoop. We went into this house. It was like 1884. The walls were covered in a dark wood panelling, a mahogany staircase led to the upper level, and one couldn't help but notice the peculiar sight of a statue which held in its upraised hand a lamp. Opening the sliding doors, I saw Russian icons and paintings, all very tasteful.

"You are so good," she told me. "I can trust you. You are a good woman/man/lady. I will pay you in advance. You will stay here. First I want to show you your bedroom at top of stairs."

She led me through a foyer where we passed through bronze gates. We proceeded up the ancient stairwell into a large room with parquet floors. A French Aubusson rug lay on the floor and a giant fox fur spread covered the bed.

"Why do you have a fox fur bedspread, may I ask?"

"In Russia, we always have fur," she explained. "Now you will come downstairs to sitting room and have champagne and you will do duty to God. The Bolsheviks come in the middle of the night. Many of them. Here is the payment in advance."

She handed me another hundred-dollar bill. That made two hundred dollars for nothing. But it really wasn't nothing—it was putting up with madness.

She crossed over to the hall and turned on the light over the statue and began pantomining a strange series of hand signals.

"Hello, hello, hello . . ."

"What are you doing, may I ask?"

"I am making an air call," she replied.

"What is an air call, may I ask?"

"Air call is much better than telephone. Telephone is no good. Air call you can talk all over the world to anyone you want."

"Really? Can anyone make an air call?"

"If you know how," she replied. "But you must have this knowledge."

"I don't have it," I told her.

"I will teach you one day," she assured me. "We will put you on a trial basis."

"Very well," I agreed.

"First we have some champagne which I promised you."

She removed a bottle of the finest champagne from the cabinet.

"You must have food," she said, opening a big tin of Russian caviar and placing some crackers in a crystal bowl.

"I will go into rear parlor where I sleep."

"Don't you sleep in the bedroom?" I asked.

"No, no, I can't sleep in bedroom."

I asked why, but she did not respond. She went in the parlor, closed the door, and I could hear the faint sound of mumbling.

I sat there and thought to myself, "What have you got yourself into?" I looked around the room and noticed a bulge under one of the sofa cushions. I put my hand there and retrieved a leather handbag. I opened it and gasped. Inside were nothing but hundred-dollar bills. I called my friend Tony Padrillo who lived across town on York and 81st Street.

"Tony, come over here!"

"No, I can't," he said. "My mother won't let me out." Tony was a fifteen-year-old queen, an escapee from Rockland State Hospital.

Since it was so late, I decided to wait until morning before I made a decision whether or not to stay with this Russian loonie. At around seven o'clock in the morning, Nina stumbled out of the parlor and began talking excitedly.

"Oh, you were so good last night! You are so strong to defend me against fifteen Bolsheviks. How strong you are. I give you bonus. I have decided you will be my protection from now on. You will move here today please."

If I had tried to protest, I probably would have been misunderstood and who knows? Perhaps she would have called the police and claimed that I forced my way into her house, stole the two hundred dollars, and I was all the Bolsheviks rolled into one tormenting her soul. So I decided, why not? I moved in that day and entered her world of madness on a daily basis. She continued to make air calls in French, German, Russian, English, Hungarian, Italian . . . She was a very learned woman and very much out of her mind. Can I survive this realm of lunacy alone? I thought. I'd have to invite friends over. One enters the world of madness by feeding on it.

I invited my friends to the townhouse. I brought Alex Ring—known as "Cherie Baby." She used to go out with a guy named Chuck Mitchell, a low-life pill freak, who later landed in jail for forging phone prescriptions. I invited Cherie to live with us. Now, Nina was quite mad, obviously, but every now and then she had moments of clarity and sanity.

"This is my friend Cherie," I announced.

"Cherie is no good," Nina affirmed. "I do not want Cherie in house. Bad evil person!"

"How can you say that?"

"No good! OUT! OUT!"

I said goodbye to Cherie. After all, fun is fun, but money is money. Before she left, Cherie asked for a shot of dope. I handed her twenty dollars and accompanied her to the front door.

"We have a good thing here," Cherie said. "She's a lunatic, but she has money!"

"We have a good thing," I said. "Yes, don't *we?*"

Cherie was bombed as usual. She looked somehow obscene in the bright sunlight, wearing a suit of men's clothing and her face full of pasty make-up. I had just taken a chippy, but was anxious for more. "Take another twenty and bring me back a hit." Twenty minutes later Cherie was back. We injected the smack and awaited the effect.

"What is this?" I exclaimed. "I don't feel a thing!"

She turned to me and said, "Nobody's perfect! I gave this cat sixty dollars for this and some downs. Here, take these Tuinals and some benzedrine. That'll get you high."

Suddenly, Nina knocked on the door. "I hear that evil man/woman here—Cherie!"

"No," I protested, while Cherie hid under the bed. "She's not here." Nina entered and immediately searched the room. She looked under the bed and pointed below. "There she is!"

"I don't know how she got in the house," I pleaded.

"She flew in the house," Nina cried. "Are you stupid?"

Nina went into the hall, brought back a broom, and began poking at Cherie. "Son of a bitch/bastard! Why you come in to bother decent woman and decent man/woman? I know who you are!"

"Do you really?" I asked. "Do you know Cherie?"

"That is no Cherie," Nina cried. "That is President Eisenhower in women's clothes! You can't fool me!"

Nina proceeded to beat Cherie out from under the bed, down the stairs, and right on out of the house. I followed behind, calling to Nina, "I'll make sure she's out of here!"

"Chase Cherie/President Eisenhower into river! Kill if you can! I pay! Kill if you can! I pay extra!"

"I'll try," I yelled, chasing Cherie away for her own good. After we were a good distance away, we stopped in our tracks. Cherie was hysterical: "She's crazy! She hurt me!"

I examined Cherie and said, "You don't need stitches. It's just a little flesh wound."

"I don't care," Cherie sobbed. "She's got money—she might have a million dollars in that house. Look at all the money she's given you."

"She's only given me a few hundred so far."

"Please let me back in there," Cherie begged.

"You can't come in. She's out for your blood!"

"Oh yeah," Cherie called as I left her. "I'll get in!"

When I got back, Nina was plopped down in her favorite arm chair, the broom upright beside her. "What happened to Cherie/President Eisenhower?"

"She ran off into the park."

"Good," Nina affirmed. "She will come back though. I know she will."

An hour or so later, the doorbell rang. Nina peeked through the curtain and asked, "What do you want?"

I scurried to the door and lifted the curtain. Cherie had a kerchief tied over her bald head (she had left her wig upstairs) and was carrying a big rubber doll, wrapped in a child's blanket, and rocking back and forth as if to soothe the baby.

"It's me," Cherie squealed.

"Vat do you want, President Eisenhower? You can't come in! No entry for you!"

"But baby is hungry," Cherie complained.

Nina suddenly took compassion on the desperate Cherie. "You have baby. Where did you get baby?"

"It's my child."

"You are too old for child," Nina said.

"This is my grandchild."

"You stole baby," Nina accused.

"Baby is hungry! It's cold out."

"I let you in only for child," Nina finally agreed. "But then you must leave. You can spend no time in my home."

She opened the door and Cherie immediately dashed upstairs. I trailed behind. "That lunatic," Cherie yelled triumphantly. "I got in, didn't I?"

"How did you get the nerve?"

Cherie told me that as she was strolling along, she passed a Goodwill shop on Columbus Avenue and spotted the big rubber doll in the window. She purchased that and an old baby blanket and made her way back to Nina's.

There was a knock at the door.

"It's me, Nina Sournin Petty. Baby is hungry and crying."

Cherie and I looked at the rubber doll. I said, "I don't hear anything."

Nina said, "Don't you hear baby crying? I give you money to feed baby. Here, give to Cherie/President Eisenhower. Tell her to buy formula."

She handed me another hundred-dollar bill.

"Thank you," Cherie cried. "Baby is so hungry!"

"Feed baby, please," cried Nina.

Nina left the doorway. Cherie turned to me and said, "I'm going to get some dope."

"Why not?" I agreed. "But this time get the real thing! Score some pills too!"

Cherie returned with thirty Tuinals, three for a dollar at the time. She brought some nickels at five dollars each and trays for three dollars of some quality heroin. We proceeded to get extremely high on heroin and Tuinals, topping it off with a touch of benzedrine. We were as high as almighty God.

I went down to the kitchen to fetch some tea when I eyed Nina in the drawing room.

"Miss/Mr./Mrs., be very careful of Cherie/President Eisenhower. She is a very bad woman/man."

"What makes you say that? She has a nice little child."

"She is very bad woman/man. She is the mistress of Boris Isnoskov, Comissar of NKVD. She is trying to assassinate me, too."

"No, that's not true," I protested.

"Oh yes! I will talk to my advisers and make air call."

Nina proceeded to make an air call in seven different languages. She then said, "President Eisenhower/Cherie must go! No one in house. She is trying to kill us. You are very strong—you must kill Cherie/President Eisenhower. I will pay you big sum of money to kill."

"Why do you want to kill her?"

"Because she is a danger to the world and to God."

"Well, God is so omnipotent and strong."

"God has his weak moments."

Oh, I thought to myself, she's playing God now.

"Very well," I told Nina. "But what should I do?"

"Kill," she commanded. "I bring you something to kill her with."

She came back with a strong axe. "Cut off head."

I looked around. "Where is she?"

Nina and I began to search the house. After some hide-and-seek,

Nina announced, "She must have escaped. President Eisenhower/Cherie knew of how we were planning to put an end to her criminal life."

"Really," I said. "Where do you suppose she went?"

"She flew," Nina determined.

"How did she fly?" I asked.

"What is the matter with you? Intelligent person—can't you see? She has evil mystic powers. She flies."

"She's very fast," I noted, looking out the window, watching Cherie in the backyard, arms loaded down with items from Nina's bedroom. She carried gold candlesticks, boxes of lapis lazuli, gold Fabergé jeweled eggs, and a handful of hundred-dollar bills which she must have discovered in one of Nina's many stashes. Engrossed in my discovery, I suddenly realized that Nina was no longer by my side. I raced downstairs only to discover Nina opening the door to the backyard.

"There is President Eisenhower/Cherie!"

"How did she get here so quickly?" I wondered aloud.

"She flew up. She flew down." Nina noticed the possessions Cherie was carrying. "Why is she taking those things? Those things are from Russia. They belonged to my family's chapel, the Russian Orthodox Church."

"Oh, I see," I said and approached Cherie. "Cherie, put those candlesticks down," I scolded.

"Do not molest her," Nina yelled.

"What?" I asked.

"Do not touch her! She has holy sanctified things. She carries the candlesticks of my family murdered by the Bolsheviks."

"But you want me to kill her," I interjected. "Mrs. Petty, did you not request the murder of Cherie?"

"You cannot kill her with those candlesticks in her hand."

Meanwhile, Cherie was frozen still and darting her wicked brown eyes back and forth from Nina to me.

"Lucky Cherie," I said softly.

Cherie flew into a rage. "Oh, fuck you, you old bitch!" She was ready to flee.

"Cherie," I demanded, "drop the shit."

"Why should I? I know who I can sell it to and make big bucks!"

Cherie was referring to a French comedienne named Blanche who had a little shop on Columbus Avenue. She had dyed henna-red hair, was painted to death, and was two days older than water. She wore sunglasses day and night, and was constantly in the company of young Puerto Ricans who she'd buy things from. You could sell Blanche anything—lost, bought, or stolen.

Cherie continued, "I can go to Blanche this minute and get a couple of hundred dollars for this shit!"

"No, no, don't be foolish," I warned.

Cherie dropped everything but the cash and sprinted.

Nina was rather calm. "We let her go. Very good. But we will get her. We will see President Eisenhower again."

"Maybe she won't come back," I said hopefully.

"No, she will be back. She has a wish on my life."

"What is that?" I asked her. "A wish on your life?"

"Last week when I made air call I was informed by Lenin, Isnoskov, and Trotsky that I would be killed by current American President."

"But Trotsky is dead," I said.

"No, he's not dead," Nina insisted.

"He was assassinated in Mexico in the 1940s," I told her.

"No, no, that's wrong. Trotsky is living around corner on 79th Street with Chinaman in Chinese laundry."

"No! Really? No one knows that!"

"Don't be stupid, Margo. I know that."

"How do you know that?"

"My people told me."

"Oh really? How come the police don't know?"

Nina became impatient. "Sssshh. I cannot hear my people and hear you at the same time. Do not speak."

"I can understand that," I said softly.

I remained silent as Nina concocted a new plan.

"Very well," she announced. "Very good! I know. We will trap her and also we will get Chinaman around the corner who is not a real Chinaman. He's making believe he is Chinaman."

"Really?"

"Yes," Nina said. "You must help me. I will pay."

"I do not want more money."

"Yes you do," she insisted. "You are a professional. And a very good one. Where did you have training? Did you train in Germany?"

What makes you say that?"

"You look Germanic."

"No, actually I was not trained in Germany."

Nina disagreed. "You were trained in German Secret Service."

She thought that I had been trained by Kaiser Wilhelm, who died in 1942 in Holland, exiled from his own country. He had sent a telegram to Hitler before his death: "I congratulate you on the victory of taking the city of Paris." He died shortly thereafter.

She was convinced that I was trained in espionage, a German spy, and would defend her from the Bolsheviks she fantasized about.

"Are you sure she's coming back?" I asked.

"Ssshh. Please," she said to me. "She has orders to come back."

"May I ask you a question?" I politely said. "Why is it so important for all these people to kill you?"

Nina hesitated a moment. "I cannot tell you. I cannot tell you. I cannot tell you."

"Very well."

At this moment, there was a banging on the door. We were upstairs, but Nina could hear a pin drop from anywhere.

"There she is," Nina whispered.

I followed Nina down the stairs. I was dressed in my charming peach-colored velveteen housecoat.

Nina looked at me. "You know who it is."

Then she opened the curtain a bit. Lo and behold, it was not Cherie, but a perky platinum blonde in a crimson silk dress, pillbox hat, and stiletto heels.

"Who is it?" I asked Nina. "Is it Cherie?"

"No, no," Nina said. "It is an angel."

"An angel?"

"A pretty and young angel," she assured me.

"Really?"

Nina swung open the door. Enter Lana, who sidled up next to me and whispered in my ear, "Margo, I heard you got plenty in here."

"What do you want, Lavin?" I asked.

"I heard you struck it rich," Lana said.

"What do you want?" I repeated.

"Let me in," he said. "I need a fix!"

"No, I'm sorry. I can't help you." Then, under my breath I said, "Begging bitches. An old woman is here."

They were making a habit of coming to me. Rayline, Maxine, Georgie, and now Cherie and Lana—all taking advantage of my kindness, my weakness.

"Who is this angel?" cried Nina.

"This is my friend," I said.

"What is her name?"

"This is Lana Turner."

"Who is Lana Turner?"

"She is an American actress."

"I never heard of Lana Turner," confessed Nina. "Never heard of. I heard of Ethel Barrymore, Madam Ospinskya, but I never heard of Lana Turner." She turned to Lana. "Are you related to Ethel Barrymore?"

"Yes," Lana said. "She's my aunt."

Nina seemed suddenly relieved. "Oh, very nice. I saw her in *Captain Jinx of Horse Marines*."

"Oh yes," Lana said. "Thank you for remembering."

"You are very nice. Are you also doing the good work?"

Lana smiled sweetly for a moment and replied, "I try."

"You will help to rescue children," Nina decided.

What next? I asked myself. "What children?" I asked Nina.

"I think sometimes you are so very stupid, Margo. Don't you know what's happening on 79th Street at Chinese laundry? Leon Trotsky and Boris Isnoskov are posing as Chinese laundrymen."

"No, what exactly is happening?" I inquired, wanting to know more.

"They are killing children. And eating them. They are cannibals.

96

Killing children and cooking and selling them in Chinese restaurants as pork."

"Really? I am shocked!" Lana and I gazed at Nina.

"You must do something about this," demanded Nina. Then, turning to Lana, she said, "Do you want to work for me, too?"

"Yes," Lana said.

Nina said, "You are too pretty to work. You are not hard enough. You are not strong enough. I'm afraid they will hurt you. But I will give you something for being so sweet."

She handed Lana a hundred dollar bill. Lana's eyes shone like the stars.

"I must go," Lana promptly stated. "I must see—about helping the children!"

So off she went to cop a hundred dollars' worth of dope.

Nina changed from minute to minute. But for some reason she always favored me. When Lana's supply of smack had run out, and her drug-dependent spirit was back in the land of dull reality, she naturally decided to return for more of Nina's generous offerings. By now, however, Nina had had enough.

"What do you want?" asked Nina from the window.

"It's me. Lana Turner."

"I know no Lana Turner," Nina insisted.

"I want to come in and see Margo."

"No, you cannot come in house. You are a bad woman/man. Man/woman at that!"

I heard Lana and came to the rescue. "You remember Lana. She's nice. You spoke to her the other day."

"Are you crazy," Nina said. "I never saw that person in my life."

She refused to open the door. Then, suddenly, a fuse blew in the cellar. The lights in the parlor turned off instantly and our normally plentiful supply of heat cut off.

"I must call plumber to fix stove. No heat and we will freeze as my family did many years ago." Nina proceeded to make the air call.

Meanwhile, I had an idea. "I have to go to the store," I told her.

"You have everything here that you need," Nina offered.

"I must get some coal for the stove to keep us warm." I thought to myself, I need some pills to get through this. When I stepped outside, I saw Lana pacing in her blue fox coat. She asked me why the old lady had changed her attitude toward her so dramatically.

"Never mind that," I said. "Look, when you come by, tell her you are the plumber. We're expecting one to fix the furnace. I think it's the fuse."

I hopped in a cab and went to see Tommy Fitzsimmon, a homosexual living on West 44th Street on the top floor of a tenement. He weighed between 385 and 424 pounds, was between forty-two and fifty years of age, and used to sit in the center of his bed and try to molest young queens who came to buy ten benzedrines for a dollar. He would try to give Tony Hietmuller and Kora Pearl and all the other young queens blow jobs for money and pills he could provide.

"I want one hundred bennies. Here's ten dollars."

I was in and out of there so fast he hadn't time to plot his seduction. I dashed back in a taxi which then cost the grand total of a dollar eighty-five. How prices rise! Getting out of the cab, I noticed that lovely Lana had arrived, this time dressed in dingy overalls. Nina was peering through the curtain, as if it was a scene from *Psycho*.

"What do you want?" she asked.

"Plumber," was all Lana said.

Here was a platinum blonde shoulder-length-haired drag queen with false eyelashes, white pancake make-up, and pink lipstick, decked out in ratty overalls under a shabby old wool coat.

"I've come to fix your stove," Lana said as Nina opened the door.

"Oh yes. You plumber. Come in. We go to cellar and fix stove. It's out of order." Nina spotted me and motioned me inside. "Plumber is here!"

We proceeded to the kitchen and Nina directed Lana down to the cellar.

Lana Lavin was a genius at fixing things, a virtuoso mechanic! She went downstairs, banged on the stove, probably more for effect, and five minutes later, a roar of heat blasted from the ventilator. Crazy Lana Lavin, drag queen extraordinaire, saved the day!

"Very good," Nina told Lana. "I hear heat coming on now. Very good job Mister/Miss/Lady/Gentleman/Plumber."

Lana just looked at her.

"I don't care. Very good job. I give you nice bonus." She handed Lana a couple of hundred dollars for what was at most a thirty-five dollar job.

"Thank you very much," Lana said, grateful for a change.

"Leave number with us. In fact, do you take air calls?"

Lana glanced at me quizzically as I nodded my head up and down.

"Oh yes. I take air calls," he said.

Nina said, "Very good. When I need plumber, I call you. You're very good."

When Lana left, Nina asked me, "That plumber, man/woman?"

"I don't know," I stated.

Nina thought Lana was a marvelous plumber, and therefore, Lana had a marvelous "in" to Nina Sournin Petty's good fortune.

I had now been with Nina over a year. Cherie, Lana, Kora Pearl, and other assorted lunatics were coming in and out. A young Polish friend of mine, Stanley, used to converse with Nina in beautiful classic Slavic. I asked him what Nina was saying during her frequent murmuring attacks. It seems as if she was lamenting her long-lost relatives in the form of song and poetry. She continued to make air calls in English, Russian, German, French, and Italian. She was old and frail, but one could easily look at her face and detect how beautiful she once was. This woman was probably, at one time, breathtakingly beautiful.

After fifteen months of this pseudo-hibernation, my drug habit was out of hand. I would seek and find hidden packets of money all over the house. Sometimes Nina would include notes: "Miss/Mr./Mrs., here is $500. Give to needy children. Find them."

But as my drug habit grew, I became more and more greedy. One day Cherie and Neal "Skippy" Mora were visiting. This was before Skippy and I were on the outs, on account of how he later tried, repeatedly, to kill me. Anyway, there was not a centavo in the house, as everything was going for heroin. We were quickly fading from our last dose, so I gathered some momentum and sought Nina out in the parlor.

"Mrs. Petty?"

"What do you want, Margo?"

"We need money for children."

"I took care of children."

"We need money for salary."

"I paid you yesterday for a month."

"No, no."

"Look, Margo, I want to talk to you."

Her mind came to a semblance of sanity. "I am not foolish woman. You are not that crazy. You have good and true heart, but you have friends who are very evil people. I know upstairs in your bedroom is very strange person with one blue eye and one brown eye."

True, Skippy had one aquamarine eye, the other brown.

Nina continued. "This is sign of possession of demons."

Skippy could be a bit nasty.

"You are so kind you do not notice. That's why I must take note for you. Also, President Eisenhower/Cherie has returned. I know they do things with narcotics."

"What?" I asked innocently.

"I know when the pupils are dilated."

"What does that mean?" I said with disbelief.

"Your pupils were dilated a few hours ago."

"No!" I protested.

"You cannot lie to me."

"What makes you say that?"

"I am not foolish. I know."

Sanity was overwhelming her.

"I like you very much," she continued. "I do not like friends you have. They are bad. I have suffered very much in my life."

"Really?" I asked. "Tell me about it."

100

"I don't like to talk about it. But you know in Russia, during the trouble, the First World War, revolution came, in 1917."

"Yes, I am aware of the Russian Revolution," I said.

"My entire family was destroyed in this revolution," she solemnly stated.

"Oh, I'm very sorry."

"I lost husband, three children, brother, sister-in-law, all nieces and nephews—all killed by the Russian Bolsheviki."

"The Bolsheviks?"

"Yes," she replied.

"Oh, how sad. How did you come to be here?"

"In 1917, I was at my family's home outside Petrograd, or St. Petersburg. We called it Petrograd at the start of the First World War. I was at our home, our country home. One day, I went for mail, but none was there. I went to my servants' quarters and no one was there. The house was empty except for me.

"I heard the horses coming. It was the Bolsheviks. They were ravaging and looting any home with money or valuables. All property they took with no mercy. I ran. I was dishevelled."

"Oh yes," I said. "I know the feeling."

"Night was coming on," Nina continued. "Day before I had birthday dinner at home. I went to sleep with my new pearl necklace on. Very long necklace, matchless Oriental pearls. I ran downstairs to back of house, wearing only necklace and silk lace negligée. No one was there. We had many, many servants, but the place was abandoned.

"They came on horse through the door. I heard the horsemen in the parlour and in sitting room. I ran into fields. I hid in the woods."

"What month was this, may I ask? Russia is very cold in winter."

Nina looked at me and said, "It wasn't that cold at the time."

"Oh."

"I saw as they burned my home," Nina told me.

"Oh really? Was this the outbreak of the revolution?"

"This was when they arrived at St. Petersburg. The government fell. It was complete madness. The worst element of extreme Russian Bolsheviki was on the rampage.

101

"I saw my country home burnt to the ground. I went to one of my peasant's homes."

"One of your peasants?" I asked.

"Then we had all this land we owned."

"You had your own peasants," I asked again.

"They gave us some of their crop."

"Oh, you mean what they call sharecropping? How much of the harvest of their farms did you receive as rent?"

"We were very fair people. Only seventy percent of what they raised."

I thought to myself, They wonder why there was a revolution in Russia!

"We were very good to our people," she continued.

"Oh, I see. How long were they there for?"

"They were there forever. We had other estates. This was not our biggest estate. This was one of the smaller ones."

"Oh."

"The big one was in the Ukraine where we had wheat."

"A bigger estate? How small was the one outside Petrograd?"

Nina thought for a moment. "It was not small and it was not large. Only a hundred thousand acres."

"The one in the Ukraine was bigger?"

"Much bigger. Many, many times bigger.

"I went to the peasants house and said, 'Help me.' They looked at me and stared. I had to show my pearls to let them see I was their superior. The old lady was loyal because I had given her a Christmas gift, a piece of material to make something nice. Very nice material. It was not cotton— it was linen. About fifteen yards. She remembered and gave me a piece of rough material which I put over me. It was very coarse. I made my way into the city of St. Petersburg.

"I had to find a way to leave the terror. It was like the French Revolution in a way. Equally bloody. It was the reign of terror in Russia in 1917. I went to the center of Petrograd, which was where we had our city palace.

"My husband was Count Igor Sournin. I was mother of three children—two boys and a girl. My father was a member of the Czarist government, assistant to Grand Duke Sergei, who was the governor of St. Petersburg.

"I went to palace and saw it, all smashed windows. Not destroyed, but broken into. I was afraid to go near. I asked a friend I knew, a doctor, middle-class, who was physician to family, where my family was. He informed me that there had been a massacre. He told me my entire family—father, mother, sister, brother, and my husband and three children were gone.

"I said to Doctor, 'Did you see them die? How do you know they're dead?'

"Doctor said, 'They are dead.'

"I didn't know what to do. I had no money, could not go to bank. Everything was looted, but I did have a pair of matchless pearls which even in those days was worth a great deal of money."

"Yes, I know what Oriental pearls cost then and now. Real is real," I said.

"I was so beside myself that I found help through someone I know who was a clergyman's daughter. In Russia, only the high bishops have celibate lifestyles. Ordinary clergy, Russian priests, can marry and have children. Bishops, however, have to remain celibate."

"I know that," I said.

"You are very smart woman/man. You know all about history.

"I went to woman who told me all of the clergy were being purged and atrocities were occuring. The Bolsheviks were burning churches. All of the families were being persecuted. They would be leaving Russia in small groups.

"I went with her and received support. We had food and lodging, but transportation was a problem. We were about twenty people, mostly women, a few old men, and decided to take train to Sibera.

"We went to Central Siberia. Winter was coming on. You know Siberia in the winter? Very cold! It was the end of train line. We had to walk to border of Mongolia. Siberia is on the border of Mongolia."

"Yes, I know my geography."

"We walk hundreds of miles. Maybe seven or eight hundred miles. We take months and months to walk and sleep, at the mercy of strangers.

"I was able to contact lawyer in Mongolia who could help me get money sent from France where my family had bank account for our summer stay in France. We always stay summer in France. I had some money there—not much—eighty or ninety thousand dollars. I had money sent to Mongolia. I had no papers, no passport. I went to Swiss Red Cross and told them I was a stateless person and they got in touch with the Swiss government, who issued me a temporary Swiss visa. I was able to travel to China.

"I went to Shanghai on this visa which would expire in six months. Shanghai was very cosmopolitan."

"Yes, I know," I said. "I shopped in Shanghai when I was a child. We used to take a ship from Singapore. It was like Paris—the Paris of the Far East. A lot of Russian people were in Shanghai."

"I took lease on house there and ran a house for men and women, a guest house with meals and lodging to make some money."

"Very enterprising," I commented and then thought, "for a Russian Countess."

"It was a moderate income. Just before 1920, after the First World War, I met very charming American who was Colonel in U.S. Army Engineers. He was from Baltimore, Maryland. His name was Colonel Joseph Petty. He was in army many years. He was maybe forty-five; I was in my thirties. I rent him room. We took up conversation. He was very charming; he was lonely. His wife had died and he had no children. I married him and became Mrs. Petty. We went to the station in China where there was American mission and left China in the early 1920s. We came to Baltimore where we lived for a few years. My husband was a professional man and his family did not have lots of money, but they were very comfortable. They had land—a little property in the city of Baltimore.

"We lived in Baltimore during the Depression. We bought this house in 1932 and lived very peacefully until second Great War around 1939. Pearl Harbor attack, the Japanese . . ."

"I'm very familiar with that," I told Nina.

"He died after Pearl Harbor. He died before Christmas, 1942. When God was sleeping, for how else could He allow these things to happen?

"You are educated well and you know all these bum/bastard/bitches who are prostitutes."

"Are they really prostitutes?" I asked.

"Yes. They do not sell what they're supposed to sell. They fool men."

Nina was all too aware of the truth.

"Oh my heavens!" I declared.

"I have great deal of money," she said. "But I do not give you money because I know what you are going to do. You want money for drugs!"

"Well," I said, "you know how the drug heroin works. You take a little—"

"Yes," she interrupted, "but you have to stop."

"But I need it!"

"No. I give you no money."

She returned to her parlour. While she was in there, I went to her desk, retrieved her handbag, reached in, and filled my pockets with hundred-dollar bills. Loads of them. I then went upstairs.

On this afternoon, about three-thirty, I was coming down the steps and caught a glimpse of Nina standing in front of the door.

I pushed her aside.

Why did she have to pick now to get so suddenly lucid and sane again?

"I don't want you to have that money for drugs," she said.

"Get out of the way," I screamed.

Then she opened the door and yelled, "Help! Help! Police!"

As it happened, a police car was passing by 78th Street and heard Nina yelling. I rushed back upstairs.

The police asked what was wrong.

Nina politely said, "How do you do? I am Nina Sournin Petty and this is my house and I have a caretaker here named Margo who is rather strange. She is man who looks like woman who is a kind person, but . . ."

"What?" the police asked.

"She pushed me today and took, I don't know how much exact, but several thousand dollars in hundred-dollar bills. I took out today five thousand dollars and I don't know how much Margo took. She grabbed my handbag and pushed me."

The police were interested. "Pushed you? This is robbery and assault."

"No assault," Nina said. "Just pushed me."

"You're an old lady. That's assault."

I slowly descended the stairs. Nina pointed at me and yelled, "You!"

I calmly replied, "What is it?"

The police shouted, "Come down here!"

"What is it?" I asked.

"You're under arrest."

My pockets were bulging with hundred-dollar bills, but luckily he couldn't see that. I had the evidence on me.

"You're under arrest for robbery and assault. Turn around."

He handcuffed my hands behind me.

"There are more of those strange people up there," Nina told him.

"Very well, Mrs. Petty, we'll arrest them then," he informed her. "You will have to go to the stationhouse to press charges."

"Very well."

"Will you get your coat? It's rather cold out."

"No, no. I don't have to," Nina protested.

I had to speak now.

"Officer, you're making a terrible mistake. I am taking care of this lady for her family. I am a psychiatric nurse. A trained specialist. The lady is mentally ill!"

"She sounds like she knows what she's talking about," the policeman said. Then he turned to Nina. "Would you get your coat, ma'am?"

"Just a moment," Nina replied. "Why should I go get coat and go out in the cold. I will talk to whom I have to talk to here."

"You have to make a complaint with the detectives at the station."

"No, no," Nina said. "I can talk to judge now. I make air call."

She proceeded to make her call in front of the mirror. Her lucidity was leaving her.

"Hello, hello judge. The Okrana [the Czarist Police] and the

Bolsheviks are here. The police are here. They have Miss/Mr./Mrs. Margo. They are getting Cherie. I wish they would take President Eisenhower/Cherie away. President Eisenhower is upstairs in women's clothes. Put President Eisenhower/Cherie, who robs the country, robs the poor, and kills the children, into the prison. Miss Margo I want you to give a little mercy to because she has a good heart. She just doesn't know because she has the bum/bitch/bastards who are bad women/men here."

The cop looked at me. "Is she going to be all right?"

"Yes, she'll be all right," I said.

The cop unlocked my handcuffs.

"Mrs. Petty, dear," I said, "it's time for your Thorazine."

I was saved by an air call. When the police left, I counted the money in my pockets. There was four thousand and-some-odd dollars.

I continued to stay with Nina. She used to make air calls out on the street by a lamppost. The police never interfered again.

One day a man came to the house. He was a Russian Orthodox priest with a big hat and a big beard. He rang the bell and knocked on the door.

I went downstairs and looked through the window. "Yes?"

He announced himself. "I am Father Peter Berushka, a distant relative of Mrs. Petty's."

"A priest?"

"Yes, I am a member of the clergy. I am with the Saint Something Church in Paterson, New Jersey. I am distantly related to the Countess. I'm very concerned because some Russian friends have sent me letters saying they are very worried about my relative's mental health. She seems to be wandering around the streets talking to lampposts and mumbling to herself."

At this point, Nina appeared with a spear in her hand. A huge African spear with a scalpel-like point on one end. She hit him with the stick end of the spear.

"What are you doing?" I cried. "This is a priest of your church. A long-lost relative!"

"He is not a priest," Nina declared. "He is Isnoskov in disguise."

The priest turned to me. "This lady, my relative, is psychotic."

"I'm here for that," I told him.

The priest said, "Who are you?"

"My name is Margo Howard-Howard."

"Margo who?"

"Margo Howard-Howard. I am a qualified registered psychiatric nurse."

"May I see your credentials?" he inquired.

"Well, I haven't got them here at the moment."

"Do you live here?"

At that time, Cherie and several other freaks appeared.

"There is something very wrong here," he continued.

"Get out," Nina yelled.

The priest looked frightened and said, "I will leave, but I will return."

Two days later, a man rang the door.

He said, "I am from the Department of Mental Hygiene."

I asked him what he wanted.

"I have an order to question Mrs. Nina Sournin Petty, as we have received many complaints of her irrational neurotic and psychotic behavior."

"She's not here," I said.

Nina had heard the man, of course. "Who is there?"

"It's no one," I lied.

"Is that Mrs. Petty?" the man called to her.

"No," I lied again.

"Yes, I am Nina Sournin Petty," Nina said, over my shoulder. "Who are you?"

I stepped aside and let the mental health officer in.

"Your name is Mrs. Petty?"

"Yes, Mrs. Nina Sournin Petty."

"May I ask your age?"

"How rude! How rude to ask a lady her age."

"Do you know what city and state you're in?" he asked.

"Of course I know where I'm at," Nina said.

"Will you tell me, please?" he said.

"No!"

"Do you know today's date?"

"Why do you want to know the date?"

"I must have these facts," he said, evidently frustrated.

"I won't give them to you. Get out!"

"I cannot leave," the poor man said, "until I ascertain some more facts."

"Get out!"

I stepped in at this time. "You better leave, sir. I'll handle it. I am her companion."

"You are a paid companion?" he asked.

"Yes."

"Who pays you?"

"Some of the family."

"She has no immediate family," he told me. "There's a Russian Orthodox priest who has petitioned the New York State Department of Mental Hygiene to investigate this case. Also, we have had some complaints. I'll have to detain her until she is mentally well enough to handle her own affairs."

"But I'm here," I said.

"What are your credentials, ma'am?" he asked again.

"Well . . ."

"I have to put your name on the register, you see."

"Margo Howard-Howard."

"A hyphenated Howard? Why's that?"

"It's exactly what it means. You see, I was born a Howard and I married a cousin who was a Howard, too."

He looked at me like I was insane, too.

Nina, at this point, came out with the African spear again and started to batter the mental hygiene official.

"Oh no," the man cried. "I'll have to send two physicians for this one."

Later, he came back with two medical doctors who looked at Nina and signed some papers. An ambulance arrived which took her away to Bellevue Psychiatric Ward.

So there I was, left with enough bankbooks to match a deck of cards, none of which I could do anything with, $10,000 in one account, $100,000 in another.

I decided to find a doctor. Dr. Solomon Rubinstein lived on Central Park West. I had looked him up in the phone book. Being the devious entrepreneur that I can be, I knew I had to get some charlatan psychiatrist who would do anything for a dollar.

I called the doctor to make an appointment.

"Yes? Therapy?"

"No, not actually therapy. I'd like to see the doctor concerning a relative who needs help."

"Very well," said the voice over the telephone. "It's thirty-five dollars an hour."

"Very well," I agreed.

"Even if you want to talk about someone, it's thirty-five dollars an hour I will charge you."

I arrived at the office of Dr. Rubinstein for my scheduled appointment. I wore corduroy pants, a big wool coat, and had my hair pulled up under my hat.

The nurse, who resembled Selma Diamond, said to me, "Thirty-five dollars."

I handed her the money.

"Your name?"

"My name is Blanche DuBois."

"Blanche DuBois? Funny! I saw A *Streetcar Named Desire*, too! You have an appointment?"

"Yes, I spoke to the doctor."

She looked at her log. "Yes, there's an appointment for Blanche DuBois." She called the doctor in.

The doctor said, "You're Blanche DuBois?"

"Well," I said modestly, "that's my theatrical name."

"You're in show business? What do you do?"

"I work as a femme mimic."

"Oh, a drag queen? You ever work in the Jewel Box or the 82 Club?"

"Well, I worked in both."

"I go to the 82 now. Do you know Kit Russell?"

"Yes, I know him."

"Oh, I love the show. What can I do for you, darling?"

"Well, doctor, I have a relative. She's elderly and she is a bit mentally ill, but I would rather have her at home."

"She's got money, huh?"

"Well, a little," I said quietly.

"Where have they got her? The state?"

"They took her to Bellevue."

"Well, I could get her out if I have an affidavit saying that she's going to be my patient and will come in for therapy and I'll be treating her with the right drugs, for her psychoses . . ."

"Yes. Will you take care of this right away? I'm very upset and distraught."

"Yes. What's it worth?"

"Well, I have some money for you now."

"How much?"

"Five hundred dollars."

"That will do for now. What's the old bag's name?"

"Nina Sournin Petty."

"Married?"

"Yes. Mrs. Joseph Petty."

"How old?"

"Well, I don't know really. Let's see, she was twenty-eight in 1917 . . . maybe eighty . . . something like that . . ."

"A relative and you don't know her age? What's the story here?"

"Well, I'm a companion to her."

"Companion." He was writing this down. "Yeah, yeah, yeah. Well, O.K. Her age doesn't matter."

He wrote "old" on his form.

Yes, we got her out. We were together once more at the townhouse, that is, until her untimely passing.

She had tried to stop a fire engine on Broadway.

"Wait a moment!" Her last words.

THE TIME SKIP MORA
TRIED TO KILL ME

18

SKIP Mora tried to kill me by pushing me out a window. Skippy was a notorious drag queen. We were bitter enemies. One time Skip had a boyfriend knock me down the stairs. I was then living at 119 West 78th Street, in a townhouse. Everyone heard I had a gold mine. He got in the building and I chased him out in the yard with the African spear.

They had no fire escapes on the building because it was a private house, but Skip managed to crawl up a drainpipe. He got on the roof and crawled to the window of my bedroom. I went out and fought with him and he almost knocked me off the roof.

There were several incidents with him. Another time he came after me with a sawed-off shotgun in a shopping bag, on Broadway and 78th Street. He walked up to me, pulled the gun out of the bag, and said, "I'm going to kill you." But I knocked the gun in the air and it went off, and it made so much noise that he dropped it and ran down the street. So I picked it up, put it in the bag and ran up the stoop. I had the shotgun for a long time. We had such bitter feuds going on. He wanted to kill me. I didn't want to kill him. It was too much trouble. He was jealous of my scene.

Eventually someone gave him a "hotshot." They gave him enough heroin to kill him. He was very unscrupulous. He was a terrible thief.

THE HOTSHOT

19

I RECEIVED overdoses several times. Once my friend Lisa, who was part white and part black, looked like a woman, and was larger than a cow, and had a very sweet, melodious voice, and I had been out selling our wares. I had about $800.

I went to the apartment of a queen called Jerry Humphreys, who was evil incarnate. He lived at 103rd Street between Central Park West and Manhattan Avenue, on the sixth floor. I bought some heroin, what they then called a couple of half loads of heroin—a dozen nickel bags, which were twice the weight and quality of what you would get today. There was a little less than a gram in each bag.

I told them not to give me too much because I was high already. They gave me enough to kill me or a horse—a herd of horses, a herd of hippopotamuses. I collapsed, dead to the world—and my "friends," the cutthroats, thought I was dead. I was unconscious, I couldn't see anything, couldn't hear anything, couldn't think, but right then and there I somehow *felt* they had given me a hotshot. Everything was getting darker, darker, as though I was falling into a black pit.

They panicked. They opened the window and threw my body out.

It was late in the morning, in summer. All the respectable people in the building had done their wash, and the laundry was hung out to dry. The clotheslines broke my fall. I woke up covered in sheets and white linen. This big black mammy who had seen my descent came running up and said, "What are you doing to my wash?"

It was the last straw for the police. They raided Humphreys' place a few days later for possession and the gang was all taken to jail. I ended up with a fractured pelvis.

Before I met the debonair, ever so charming Mister Barnes, I would go to various dens around town to get my heroin. There was a hotel on Broadway between 74th and 75th Street, with tiny little rooms and cubbyholes. Now it's a very glamorous building. You could tell that at one time it had huge apartments but the apartments had been broken up into tiny little rooms. It was a hellhole. They had little community kitchens in the hall. Most of the people in the building were addicts, and the sale of heroin went on there; you got what you needed with a couple of dollars.

Legalization of drugs has its virtues as well as its detriments. Look at how well it worked in England—they don't have as much addiction there. It's government-controlled. They give them heroin, they give them methadone, they give them anything they want. Then people don't have to worry about being robbed, because the addicts get it from the government.

TRUMAN AND ME

20

THE ADVENTURES which involved my various friends and me are countless, yet there is a particular episode that stands out in my mind.

I met Truman Capote in the year of our Lord 1961. It was a fall afternoon and I was wearing a thin tweed suit, a ranch mink stole, and a charming pillbox hat. Jack Kennedy was putting in his bid for the presidency and Jacqueline Kennedy was around showing off her wardrobe and I was lucky enough to share similar tastes. In my hand, I carried a lovely alligator handbag. I wore black leather gloves and black leather shoes. I was feeling quite well that afternoon. In other words, I had just shot a jumbo dose of crystalized meth, which does tend to make one rather hyperactive.

I had just lunched with Mr. Saul Hite. As I strolled down Fifth Avenue, just as I was passing the Hotel Pierre, I noticed, lo and behold, a spectacle ahead which one simply could not miss—a little plump munchkin carrying a cane.

I recognized him immediately as Truman Capote.

Being the kind and gracious lady that I can be at times, besides the bitch that I am the rest of the time, I said, "Mr. Capote, is it?"

"Yes," he replied.

"How do you do?"

"Fine. Do I know you?"

"No, I have not had the distinction of meeting you before, but I've always admired you."

"Thank you," he said. "What is your name?"

"Margo Howard."

"Do I know you?" he asked again. "I know a lot of people. Who's your husband?"

"My husband you wouldn't know."

"Are you sure? You're not in show business, are you?"

"No. I'm not."

He thought, since I was dressed so well, that I was a society lady.

"What can I do for you, dear?"

"It's nothing you can do for me," I stated. "I just wanted to tell you how much I admire you."

"Thank you. You're very kind."

"Oh yes, one of the first books I read was one of your first books, *Other Voices, Other Rooms*, which I was very thrilled with."

"Thank you, thank you. You're so nice."

"Yes, I've always admired you. You're such a great writer. And your new book *Breakfast at Tiffany's* that just came out. It's such an astronomical wonder. You blend reality and fiction and it's a unique thing for a writer to do. I do a little dabbling myself in writing."

"Oh, that's very nice. Thank you so much. It's so nice to meet you."

"Yes. Now, before you go, I want to tell you something else. I'm like you are."

"You're what?"

"I'm like you are—gay."

"What?"

"I'm gay."

"Oh. You have a beautiful speaking voice." He seemed confused. "You're a nice lady anyway."

"You're a nice person, too. But I'm trying to tell you that I'm like you because I'm gay."

"What does that mean?"

"I will tell you in confidence. Being an admirer of yours—I'm a man like you are. I'm a drag queen."

"What?"

"I'm a drag queen! A man in woman's clothes."

"*What?* What do you mean?"

"I mean, that I'm a queen, like you. I'm a man."

"What do you say?"

"I say what I mean."

He looked at me quizzically, then his mood turned to annoyance. He said, "It's people like you that make it so very hard for homosexuals in the world. Deceiving and confounding and confusing people. That's why we have as hard a road in America as we do in the rest of the world. You should be dead. You're a disgrace!"

"What are you saying? What are you talking about?"

"I'm saying that you're better off dead. Someone like you has no right to live!"

"You little fag bastard! I'm taking the edge off you. I'll teach you what a real drag queen's like!"

I took my shoes off, and stood there in my silk stockings (the chauffeur was still holding the door as Truman Capote had just about entered the car). I leaned back, my handbag in my hand, and threw a punch like a professional boxer. I knocked him into the car, he turned upside down, his feet flew in the air, and he hit his head on one of the windows.

A gash appeared on his head; he was bleeding all over the place.

"Oh my God," he yelled. "Help, police, help!"

I looked at the chauffeur. "And you, what are you going to do about it? You don't know what I have in this handbag. I might have a gun, a knife, or a bomb."

The chauffeur replied, "I'm not interested ma'am." (He called me ma'am!) This Irish-American driver said, "I am only here to drive Mr. Capote to the airport. This is a hired limousine service."

I said, "Take that bitch to the hospital first! She's bleeding! She needs stitches."

He said, "It's not my affair. I will take him where I have to take him."

He didn't know what kind of lunatic I was, after all.

I slipped my leather shoes back on and made my way down Fifth Avenue. After a few minutes, I heard the wailing of an ambulance trailing from somewhere behind me.

EARNING POCKET MONEY

21

TO EARN pocket money, I went out with men. So one time I went out with this gentleman who worked for Unitog in St. Louis, Missouri. They made industrial uniforms for factories all over America. I met him on Central Park South, at about seven o'clock in the evening, near the St. Moritz Hotel. He called out to me, "Oh, Rose!" from an outside table at the Café de La Paix. He presumed that I was a bona fide female. He stood up and said, "Oh, I'm sorry, I thought you were somebody I knew. You look so much like Rose McLaughlin from Missouri." I looked at him and I said, "Oh, that's quite all right." He was very handsome too. About thirty-five. So he said, "Would it offend you if I offered to buy you a cocktail?" And I said, "Well, no, I was just on my way out to dinner." I gave some name like Blanche Something. So we had dinner. He was drinking heavily. I was drinking heavily. He said, "I don't want to offend you, but what would the tariff be?" I said, "Oh, you have the wrong impression. I'm not a professional woman. I like you. I'm a bit of a nympho but I'm not a professional. I wouldn't take money from anyone." I could see a look of distrust in his eye. "Oh no," I said, "I couldn't do that." I didn't want to take fifty dollars off him. I wanted to rob him. I needed to get his defenses down. So I told him I lived with my aunt and couldn't bring him there. We soon were having dinner in a very nice restaurant, having a very sumptuous meal. Then he took me dancing at the Stork Club. I still have the photograph of us dancing there. Then, at about two-thirty in the morning, he said, "I'm staying with associates at the Waldorf Towers. Would you like to come spend the night?" I said, "I'd love to."

We got there and there were four of them and they were drunk as well. I was literally holding him up. They had two reception rooms and four bedrooms. We were all slurry, all drinking, all so drunk. I danced with them, and one by one they started passing out. They were feeling my legs, and they thought they were feeling my pussy—but they didn't feel anything through the panty girdle. My deception, my grand deception. Finally, my date collapsed right on the couch, unconscious. They were all out. He had on a lovely Cartier watch with a wrist alarm, which I still have. I have it re-conditioned every year. It's 14 karat gold with an alligator band. I couldn't get their rings off, but I took their watches and wallets. I saw a flight bag and emptied it out. I put their cashmere sweaters in there too. I kept calling their names, "Bill! Jack! I want to go!" but they were dead to the world.

I had a friend called Frank Kendall, who was a master paperhanger, a master of forgery, and the next morning I rang his bell on West 76th Street, and we went shopping with the stolen credit cards.

The first day we were on East 57th Street and I went to a fur shop called Gunter Jaekel. It was a very, very posh fur shop. I went in there and I saw a broadtail jacket. It was like $2900. I went to purchase it, and they called up on the phone, and those fellows hadn't yet reported the robbery. "Oh yes, Mr. Smith," they said. "You may buy anything you want. You have unlimited credit." So we went shopping all over town for days. And then the cards were reported stolen, and here is how we found out.

We went to a camera shop two days later—the first day the fools were so drunk and crocked they didn't even know what they were missing. By noontime we had thousands of dollars' worth of dresses and clothes. Frank bought wristwatches and things, everything, and on the second day we went to a lovely camera shop on Madison Avenue at about 56th Street. We were there signing the American Express form, and we saw one clerk signal to another. The other man went and stood with his back to the exit, a big glass door. And the first clerk said to us, "This card has been reported stolen. I'm going to have to retain it and detain you until the police arrive." And he got on the phone and called for the police.

I went to the door and the man guarding it said to me, "You can't leave the store." "Oh God," Frank moaned, "I need a shot." We were terrified, and I said to Frank, "What are we going to do?" He had no idea.

So I said to the clerk, "Are you going to get out of the way? Are you going to move from that door, goddammit?" and he said no.

"You don't know what I have in my handbag," I said.

"Girlie, anything you got in that handbag I can handle," he said. The bastard.

I had nothing in the handbag but a hairbrush. I took the hairbrush out and he laughed. I was seized with panic, and I backed up about four feet and took a running leap and jumped at him with all my might, and he smashed right through the closed glass doors backwards. Frank Kendall was standing there in shock, not moving, like a fool. I grabbed him by the hand and stepped over the guard's chest. The guard was bleeding all over. I said, "Don't step on his head." And we got out, ran to the corner, and got away. The police must have been a block away by that time.

Then another time I met this man on 72nd Street and Broadway in the afternoon. Went with him. Got his wallet too. Went to his apartment. He lived on Riverside Drive in the 70s. He went to his bedroom and I grabbed his wallet from his jacket and ran out the door. I got his credit card and it was a depositor's card for Macy's. Frank and I went to Macy's stores all over the city and the suburbs. We went to Macy's White Plains and we bought a few things and suddenly a man of color and a woman of color, a big fat woman, came over and said, "Store security. We want to talk to you about your depositor's account." Kendall ran out of the store and left me there. So I made a little dash for it, and the black man grabbed me and I fell on the floor and started screaming—this is in 1961, remember—and I screamed, "Help! Help!" and onlookers thought this black man was attacking me. But he flashed a badge, and took me by the arm into the security room. There the guards asked me my name. I made up something. They looked at the name on the card I was using and asked how I knew Mr. Smith. Apparently he hadn't yet reported the card stolen. I said, "Well, he's a john of mine. He's a trick. I'm a prostitute.

I'm a first-class call girl." And they said, "Well, we cannot allow you to take these purchases with you because he's overdrawn his account. You may leave."

I said, "How dare you?"

They said, "What is your connection with him? Are you his wife?" And I said, "No. If his wife knew this she would die. I'm a first-class call girl." They let me go, so as not to embarrass "Mr. Smith."

We used to take the "purchases" back for a refund. "This was a gift," I'd say. We used to buy toasters and turn them in for cash. Macy's always did give cash.

Kendall is dead. He turned respectable and started working in a state hospital as a therapist. Unfortunately, he was still indulging in drugs and he took too many and died accidentally. It wasn't on purpose, you know. Frank Kendall. Very nice. Very charming.

My life of crime was very sordid and very criminal, but I'm not ashamed of it because I had to do it at the time.

HOW I WAS SHOT

22

I WAS shot by a princess, and that was a horrible experience. This was just at the end of 1963. I met this women called Nadine, Princesse de Polignac of De Polignac champagne. She was a diplomat. I met her, again, in the Village. She was a rather strange person. She was a mannish woman who would go out in men's clothes and take me in women's clothes out in the evening as my escort. She put up her long hair and put a stocking cap over it, and then put a man's wig over that. She was a mistress of disguises, and she said she was fascinated with me and she wanted to marry me.

I was thinking about doing it because, again, of greed. She got all the drugs. She was the French cultural attaché in New York. I went a few times to parties with her. She wanted to marry me and I said yes, I'll marry you, but we have to have a pre-nuptial agreement. She took umbrage at that. She was living, then, down around the UN. I was in her apartment one day and she was taking a lot of drugs and she said, "When are we going to get married?" I said, "Well, when you've signed an annual income over to me." And she said, "That's an insult. I'll support you." But I said, "I don't want support. I want the money."

We started arguing and she said, "Who do you think you are? I am a princess of France." I said, "You're not a royal princess. You're only a princess of the realm of France, and not a royal princess anyway." She said, "I am a de Polignac of France." I said, "So what?" She said, "I am a direct descendant on one side from Talleyrand." I said, "Oh, fuck Talleyrand, he's a fool too. A defrocked bishop." So we had an argument.

I said, "I'm leaving." She said, "You're not going anywhere." I said, "Yes I am." "Oh no you're not," she said. "If you are leaving, you're going to leave in bad shape." And she went into her bedroom, and when she came out she had a pistol in her hand. She pushed me and I pushed her back. And she aimed the pistol and said, "Now you're going to get it. I'm not going to kill you. I'm going to cripple you." And then she shot me once in the hip, once in the knee. The force of the bullet spun me around like a top, and I fell on the floor. She was going to shoot me again and I gathered my inner strength and managed to grab the pistol out of her hand and just held onto it. The police came and were banging on the doors. They couldn't open them and had to smash through the service entrance. There were suddenly dozens of police running around, asking what had happened. I said a mad woman tried to murder me and they told her she was under arrest but she said, "I'm not going anywhere," and she went into the den and came out with her papers. She said, "I am a diplomat. I have diplomatic immunity." She got away with it.

I went to the hospital and the bullet had broken my pelvis. I was in the hospital for months. But I got my revenge—I wrote a letter of protest to the French Foreign Office, and she was recalled. Then she was in France, and a few years later she married the Prince de Broughily, so now she's a double princess, a princess by birth and a princess by marriage.

She liked young girls. Very young. And she was intrigued by drag queens. She would go up to Puerto Rican women in the street and say, "Can you rent me your daughter?" She would go to seedy places to find young girls of color. She was sick. I got over that too. I was in the hospital for over three months. I had a pin in my hip, with weights on it.

I did get back at her, though. I smashed her nose with the pistol. Later, I read about her marriage in the *Times*. "Champagne Heiress Marries." It was in all the papers. Her mother was from that Hennessey family of France.

It's an on-going soap opera, isn't it? She's eighteen years older than me, so now she's seventy. An old French grande dame of seventy. She had a big huge nose. Some of the French people have such big noses. De

Gaulle, de Bergerac. She was so proud. "It's people like you," I said, "who started the French Revolution."

Three months in the hospital, and I kicked the drug habit. They had to give me drugs for my withdrawal. Then I got back on junk again when I got out.

So that is the story of Nadine. I'm a survivor though, you see.

I got onto heroin by being foolish, by wanting to indulge in a substance I was attracted to. A little young shit, now dead, named Roy Damian, from Boston, a shanty Irish piece of shit, who was very handsome and very young, got me on heroin. You do things and you can't say you're sorry you did them. I'm not ashamed of it. I did it. I regret it. It was foolish, stupid, irresponsible, a very bad decision. I'll never do it again.

It is history. You can't re-direct history. Historically, how would it be if there were never an American Revolution, if we were still English subjects? How would it be if Marie Antoinette never got her head chopped off and the French Revolution never happened? How would it be if Mary Stuart didn't get *her* head chopped off? You can't go back and change history. You have to live with it. I made some terrible errors, I did some terrible things. I did some horrible things which I should be ashamed of, but I'm not.

I used to go out in the afternoons when I was living on the Upper West Side—after the Russian lady, I didn't have that income coming in any more—I was living on West 74th Street in a wonderful apartment one flight up with a lunatic landlady, 38 West 74th, between Central Park West and Columbus, a beautiful white stone building, where you came into a marble hall with a spiral staircase and a lift going up one flight. And I had a big huge room that was once a ballroom. A one-room apartment, and a tiny little bathroom, and no stove. A hot plate. Ceilings covered with gold leaf. I painted it all black. This was just before I moved in with Nicky Barnes.

I would need a fix each afternoon. I had no money. I dressed modestly. Very little make-up. A modest dress, a raincoat. I'd go to local banks. Go in and watch elderly women make withdrawals. These old Jewish women would go there and take money out and put it in their handbags. Then I would follow them, and as they'd go into their apartment buildings I'd go in the hallway, and smile, and grab their handbags. Sometimes if I had to fight for it I would push an old seventy-five-year-old woman on the floor. That I should be ashamed of, but I'm not. I had to do it for the heroin.

They would scream and rant and rave. I could hear them as I was hurrying down the street. Hear them still screaming. That's a horrifying thing. I regret that terribly. I would change that if I could. That was my greatest crime, beating up on those elderly women.

When you need heroin nothing matters, you are so crazed. If my mother wouldn't give me money I would have knocked her on the floor, too. I'd grab my own mother's bag. I needed the fix. The body is so tense, you think if you don't have it you are going to die. It's a physical pain. It's like every bone in your body is broken and sore. You start contorting your hands like you have arthritis. You have to put them in your pocket. It's like an alcoholic having the DT's. Unexplainable horror. And then when you get the heroin, that first shot—the body would take it but you wouldn't be high. Five bags, ten bags of heroin, the body was craving for it. You just feel calm, relaxed, but not high. You'd need more to get high. And then you're oblivious to everything. You're in a world of your own. People could talk to you and have a conversation but nothing is registering, and they think you know what you're saying but you don't know what you're saying. It's like the world is yours. You're the empress goddess of the world. Everyone's at your command. It's a megalomania trip. To me, the feeling was not one of peace but rather more uncomfortable. Ruler of the world but at the same time a gut feeling that you knew this was wrong—what were you doing to yourself? This is not reality. There was always fear. The waste. A mental death wish. I hoped I would die from it.

Different heroin addicts have different highs, but mine was that I felt so oblivious of everything, nothing could penetrate, but in my gut my consciousness was still there, even when I was robbing old ladies or hitting men.

A WHITE SLAVE
IN HARLEM

23

LIVING with Leroy, the then-kingpin of drugs, was not as glamorous as I thought it would be. Of course I was Nicky Barnes' hidden secret paramour long before he became the Great Black Dope Czar Legend of New York. I had him in tears at one point, tears like those a teenage girl would have for her first crush. He visited me once or twice a week, usually at six or seven o'clock in the morning. I lay there dormant, wondering when my next shot would be, in a continual fog of drug dependency. Leroy stayed with me only a few hours, and then was off to his next freaky indulgence. I was forbidden fruit, an offbeat sexual thrill who was barely known to anyone. Soon I became a threat to his machismo, and often he'd choose to stay away, sometimes for weeks at a time.

A large fat black woman, Gladys, was the servant who fed me the injections. She took loads of heroin. She lost her nursing license by stealing drugs from patients in hospitals. "I have lots of white tricks, Miss Margo," she would say to me. "I am the queen of mammyism." I asked, "What in the hell is mammyism?" She said, "That's where white men like to get degraded by a big, fat, ugly mammy like me." And men would pay for that. "It's S&M, honey," she would say. "They want a big, funky, foul, smelly bitch like me to sit on their faces and curse them." That was Gladys.

My bedroom was Nicky's bedroom too, but he came mostly after four o'clock in the morning and left by six in the morning. He came sometimes once a week, sometimes five times a week, depending on his libido. I wasn't the only one. There were other drag queens in other places too. I met one of them, black and Hispanic, named Josephine Baker after the famous chanteuse. She worked in shows, but she couldn't speak English. She lived on Edgecomb Avenue, another hideaway.

My bedroom was very pretentious. It was more than one hundred square feet, very big, and it had two beds, twin beds with canopies very high up. The beds had nineteenth century steps going up three steps. There were paintings—nineteenth century primitives, good ones; some very good prints. He didn't have good taste but he had friends who did. The walls were beige, honey-beige, very tasteful.

In the morning, I wouldn't get out of bed first thing. I'd have a shot of heroin—my arm was always out and I'd yell "Gladys, Gladys, get your ass in here. I need my shot." I wouldn't think of getting up to go to the toilet to spring a leak, take a piss. It was more like coming out of a coma, and I would have the pains of coming out of that drug-induced sleep, that craving. I could never afford this kind of habit on my own. So I'd get my shot, roll out of bed, jump down, and I'd look in the big, fabulous, gilt pier glass nineteenth century mirror. I'd go, "Oh God." I was as thin as a broom, a stick. I was emaciated. Horribly thin. Perhaps 120 pounds. I wasn't eating. I'd crave things like YooHoo sodas. Sweet potato pie. Barbecued ribs ordered out from Harlem restaurants. I literally never set foot outside the door.

Maybe it would be one o'clock in the morning, maybe five o'clock when I needed another shot.

That was my only excuse for getting up. I was mentally, morally, and not quite physically dead.

After I looked in the mirror in the morning I would call for a shot. God knows how many I had in a day. It was perpetual. And after a while I would look in the mirror and I would look beautiful, less than a minute after I thought I looked like a dog.

I couldn't focus on anything. I was just high, in a state of euphoria, twenty-four hours a day. At the same time, I guess as a result of the Jesuit education, I knew somewhere there was a tiny atom of decency. I said, "Oh God, what am I?"

My veins were shot but Gladys was wonderful about finding fresh ones. She'd say, "Oh, that's all burnt out, that's all burnt out," and she'd find another one. She would find veins all over.

The day would go on like this. I had protection there, too. Lily was appointed to me to protect me against holdups. The people on the street knew this was one of Nicky Barnes's pads. Rivals might want to hold him up.

It was unreal. I was in my own artificial world doing my own thing, which I knew was not an answer, which I knew was a death wish.

I was a non-person, barely relating to anyone. I held up my arm, rose to relieve myself, and talked about nothing. I was wasting away.

Leroy revealed little about himself. He spoke of his mother as a strong, determined woman from the Carolinas who had married a common laborer and convinced him to move to Chicago, a land of opportunity, especially for blacks. Both parents had limited schooling.

Highly secretive, Leroy covered up his secret tendencies by displaying a macho image and insisting he was anti-gay. He'd prove his machismo by hanging out with a host of female beauties, including but not restricted to his wife, Theresa. Theresa was often left alone in Cherry Hill (New Jersey) with the children while Leroy would gallivant around with various women at clubs like Count Basie's, opened by the great trumpet player at the height of his popularity. A brass rail lined the lobby, customers sat in plush velvet chairs, and elegant chandeliers fashioned the ceiling. It could have been Liberace's foyer. All the big names in jazz played there. Leroy proclaimed one unbreakable rule to the minions in his drug empire: "Don't get involved with fags." What a hypocrite! He, who had a legal wife, children, and a mistress for show, disregarded his own rule. He was an amazing con artist who beat almost every charge in New York State's penal code. It was, in comparison, a rather simple trick to keep me hidden away. While he was putting on this masterful show for an adoring black community, lurking undercover were all of his secrets, one of which was that Leroy was a man who hated women. He'd tell me on more than one occasion, "I have to call that stick bitch, Terry. I hate her, but I have to be

131

seen with her." He kept Terry happy in a $250,000 home in Cherry Hill. Leroy, not about to deprive himself, had fast foreign sports cars, diamond rings, flashy gold chains, absurdly expensive leather apparel, and, of course, apartments and homes all over the metropolitan area. That was the public Nicky. The private Nicky, however, was a freak among freaks.

We engaged in every low sex act there is. I had to play an awful dominatrix to satisfy Mr. Barnes. He called me his "Great White Goddess." His capacity for self-humiliation during our bedtime practices was unprecedented. Some of the homosexual bondage practices he made me indulge in were quite a shock. I had no idea a person could receive so much pleasure from what seemed to be so much pain. I have never before or since participated in such bizarre and deviant rituals. This fetishism was Leroy's territory. I always thought Crisco Oil was for frying or baking purposes.

When Leroy was not at home, which was the majority of the time, I kept myself floating high on heroin, and paid little attention to the environment around me. Occasionally I would glance out the window, Harlem stretching far below me. Servants (called soldiers) would bring me meals, drinks, cigarettes, magazines, and as much heroin as I could take. I was in a sub-human condition.

My friends were uncertain where I was living. Rumors abounded, but even if someone had been suspicious of my Harlem residency, they would not have dared seek me out. I developed a feeling of camaraderie with the late Anne Frank. I was alone in a certain kind of paradise, but nothing can last forever.

It must have been something about my make-up, my generally desperate appearance that clued Leroy on to the fact that I needed to be freed. Drug paradise was killing me. I began to have strong doubts and apprehensions about what I was doing living in drug-infested hibernation. Leroy was extremely perceptive and asked me what was wrong. I informed him of my decision to leave. He broke down. I never before saw a man cry over little old me before. I saw the weakness behind all the macho stance. I could not be moved; I would not be moved. He was acting like a frightened, unsure little boy.

Just before I left Lenox Terrace, I finally met the one and only

Theresa Barnes. I popped out of my room to take a look at her. We exchanged few words. "I wanted to see what you look like," she told me. I repeated that same desire to see her. Neither of us were jealous. We were two heroin addicts pinned to the same provider. She was the show piece and I the hidden vice. There was no jealousy, rivalry, or hatred between us. Theresa kept a tidy and elegant home for her precious family in one of the finest residential sections in New Jersey. I remained languid in bed, a pathetic plaything, a wasted white slave in Harlem.

Leroy's name became prominent in the 1970s and, in fact, he eventually became an unfortunate role model for poverty-stricken black children. The man who had stored me away as his hideaway mistress was now crowned "Mister Untouchable" in a cover story for *The New York Times Magazine*. He was established as Harlem's biggest drug dealer at a time when drugs were more popular than ever. A naked harem of drug-cutting female slaves, an army of tough drug "salesmen," and King Leroy were responsible for altering and drastically wounding the lives of countless victims of the drug phenomenon.

Leroy continues to get his name in the papers to this day. He made front page news in the New York *Daily News* a week before the 398th Anniversary of Mary Stuart's death (February 1985). The headline read: "He Runs Harlem's Drugs Through Jail." The same week *Time* printed a photograph of Leroy with a hood over his head to cover up his "new facial appearance." Apparently, plastic surgery was used to disguise Leroy to protect him from his old comrades.

Leroy's supreme moment of fame, however, came in September 1985 when he was featured on "60 Minutes." His face had been slightly altered, but it was easy to see that it was the same Leroy I had known (and whose heroin I loved a decade or so earlier). Mike Wallace, with his usual charming candor, held nothing back when he boldly asked Leroy, "Have you ever killed anyone?"

Leroy, with a slight pause for effect, told Mr. Wallace that he was not directly responsible for a murder, well, not exactly.

"Had other people do it for you?" Wallace asked.

"I guess that would best describe it," replied Leroy.

After serving four years in prison, Leroy was getting a bit restless. He soon discovered, through various sly detection systems, that his two main squeezes, Thelma and Shemucca, were hanging out with some of his colleagues. This was against the family codes of honor. He decided that the only way to get even would be to inform on his old pals and give them a taste of jail life. Leroy's plan was a great success. Not only did he punish his pals, but he saved his own skin as well. There is now a strong possibility of his early release from jail. Leroy, soon to be released from jail and protected by the Federal Witness Protection Program, will still not be a truly free man. However, he will breathe a little fresh air and eat a little better.

I've got a great plan for Leroy in his new life. How about his transforming himself into the ultimate disguise—a woman? I even have a grand name for him—Nicola "Edna" Barnes. We could make him an Honorary Member of The Mary Stuart Society, one of the first black members. Well, Leroy, isn't that the least I can do for you?

LEAVING DRUG PARADISE

24

THINKING things over after four years' tenure—four years *is* four years—
I thought, My God, Robert, Miss Margo, you're a Howard and a Chanler
and you haven't read a book in four years or even a newspaper except the
tacky *Enquirer* or some such madness, one of those pornographic homosexual pieces of rubbish that the gentleman of color, aka Nicky Barnes
(who was nothing but a horrible drug trafficker peddling drugs and
poisoning the youth of America), had lying around.

I said to myself, You might as well take enough heroin to kill
yourself, bitch, bastard, or whatever—or jump out the window and splash
your body all over the place, from the balcony of the Lenox Terrace
Apartments, so Percy Sutton and Basil Patterson and Shirley Chisolm and
all of the other nob-bobs can see this white lady/man aka drag queen lying
splattered on the pavement!

I sprung up from the bed as if from a nightmare: No! I grabbed a
copy of *The Amsterdam News* that one of the peons had brought in and
began reading. There were articles about the local Harlem scene, photos
of local merchants, and advertisements geared to the black community.
One ad in particular caught my eye. It was in a box with flowers and a
large cross with lines representing rays of light emanating from it. It read:
"The blessed Handmaids of Mary are now helping drug addicts, including
juveniles with no place to go and other children of God who have

unfortunately fallen prey to the evil ways of mankind." A phone number was given but no address. I knew this was a sign. I had to leave then. I went to the front door for the first time in four years and tried the handle. It would not turn! It struck me as truly bizarre that I was trying to get out of this apartment which I had been in for four years never even imagining that I would not be able to leave. I truly thought my tenure must be up. I felt like I might as well be dead. I became desperate. As I was shaking the doorknob, thoughts ran through my head: What is this life? It was a very luxurious apartment I was in, yet to be in here trapped constantly for all these years? I may as well take enough heroin to kill four horses! I stepped away from the door and seated myself momentarily on a plush green velvet chair. I will call the Sisters of the Congregation of the Blessed Handmaids of Mary, I thought. They will help me and I will be saved. I again tried the door. It would not budge. I would have to find a key. I tiptoed into Leroy's bedroom, made sure the coast was clear, and snooped around for the key which would set me free. I tried various drawers in his desk and bureau. Nothing. I was about to enter his closet when I heard footsteps approaching. I panicked and crawled under his bed. From underneath, I could see the pink slippers of Gladys, and heard her dump a giant bag of laundry on the bed. Then Willy came bouncing into the room to call Gladys to the door. Apparently, the charity folks were at the door, collecting for some cause or another. Gladys answered the door, came back into Leroy's room, walked in the closet, and went back out to offer her contribution. At this time, I quickly crawled out from under the bed and stepped into the closet before Gladys could get back. I turned on the light in the giant closet, began searching various pockets for the key, but found instead a huge sum of cash and took at least ten or fifteen one-hundred-dollar bills. I also found a nice bag of uncut heroin and took that as well. I raced out of the closet, out of Leroy's room, and into the hall bathroom. When I heard Gladys pass, I opened the bathroom door a crack, jumped out of there, and raced to the front door. I reached for the doorknob and, at last!, triumph! Gladys had neglected to bolt the door.

It was rather late at night and I was dressed in only a thin nightgown and my ranch mink coat over it. I was frightened that I would see one of

Leroy's entourage, so I decided I would walk down the stairs. I thought to myself: Where am I going? What am I doing?

Why, I was going to the Handmaids of Mary. I left Lenox Terrace forever. I was on the road to becoming human again.

Once outside, I called the nuns from a pay phone.

A sweet voice answered: "Handmaids of Mary. Our office hours are—"

"Ooohhhh," I moaned, "I'm ill. I need help!"

"Where are you," the voice calmly replied.

"I am near Lenox Terrace!"

"We are at 15 West 124th Street off Fifth Avenue by the park. We'll help you. What is your problem? Why are you so hysterical?"

"I'm a drug addict! And I'm trapped! And a white woman!"

But I was not quite a white woman of course.

The Handmaid said, "Sir, ma'am, or whatever . . ."

How gay for a nun to say that. I mean, this was 1969. Was it possible that people, even those of the cloth, were considering such things? Had the world changed that much in just four years?

"Wherever you're at," she continued, "Come over immediately. We'll help you."

So I went to the street and tried to hail a taxicab. I don't know if it was my color, my dress, or the look of panic in my eyes, but I could not stop a cab. It was very late, very cold, and I knew that I had better make tracks if I was going to save my life. I walked from 135th Street to 124th Street and from Lenox Avenue over to Fifth Avenue, about fourteen blocks. Fourteen walking blocks when I had not moved more than twenty yards at a time in Leroy's apartment. It was cold, so I did walk quite swiftly. The shot of heroin kept me going, and by the time I reached the convent, I was devastated. I rang the bell of the convent. There to greet me was, I thought, a man in a coif—or an ape in a nun's outfit. It was a woman, but I could not tell. I'm very suspicious that everyone is as debauched and debased as I am. I thought, She looks like a gorilla in drag. She was so big and had shoulders like a fullback!

She spoke: "Hello, I'm Sister Incarnata. Are you the lady who called?"

"Yes, I am."

"Please come in," she said.

It was now about four in the morning. To enter a convent at this time is not the most popular thing to do in America, or in the world, for that matter.

I went in and she said, "Please come with me," and led me to a parlor that had couches and a fireplace, quite smart for an order of black nuns. It was well-decorated with a big crucifix on the wall and a black Jesus statue and a picture of a black Virgin Mary surrounded by black saints; the aura of the Church of Rome was there in an all-black motif. The paintings, the candles, the statues, and all that.

"Can I get you something?" she offered.

"Get me a Yoo-Hoo!" I cried.

A Yoo-Hoo is a chocolate drink which was very popular with drug addicts. Chocolate is a substitute for many wonderful things in a normal frame of mind. For a junkie, however, it is standard fare.

"I don't know if we have Yoo-Hoo, but we have milk and chocolate syrup and I can make you a chocolate milkshake."

"Please!"

"Yes. Mother Augustine will see you shortly." She excused herself to fetch the milkshake.

Mother Augustine was the Mother Superior of the convent at the time. I sat there shaking and anticipating God knows what next to come and greet me. Out came another huge woman, another gorilla look-alike, who spoke to me in the softest voice I had ever heard in my life. Melodious, so melodious . . .

"Oh, hello," she said, "How are you?"

I stared at her, the sweat beading on my face and body.

"What can we do for you, darling?" she asked.

"I am a drug addict!" I hollered again. I needed a shot badly.

"Take it easy." She reassured me and sat beside me. "Have you seen your family?"

"NO! Why do you ask about my family? I haven't seen them in five years!"

My whole body was shaking. I spat the words out of my mouth. The Mother Superior took my hands and held them down in my lap.

"Well, they might think you're dead," she said. "Wouldn't it be nice to call your family in the morning?"

"No," I protested. "I don't want to!"

I was quite perplexed. "It's too much. I don't want to involve them."

"Oh, but it would be such a relief to them. They must think you're dead. Not to know is such a terrible, awful thing. This could be like a resurrection."

I thought to myself, Religious wishful thinking, but in reality they'd say, 'Who is this freaky drag?'

"Well," I confided, "I need a shot of heroin."

I reached in my lap for the dope and the paraphernalia. She saw the heroin and was crazed.

"Let me dispose of that," she said. "We don't want to have to go through legal channels."

"What legal channels are you talking about? If I don't take this now, I'll die right on this lovely checkered couch and then you might have to worry about legal channels!"

Much to her chagrin, she allowed me to inject myself. Then she insisted on disposing of the rest of the kilo or two. I imagine she must have flushed it down the commode. Uncut heroin—it must have been worth tens of thousands of dollars. The shot calmed my nerves, but I was still very confused. I was rather disgusted with myself. I had been in Harlem for four years without leaving the apartment and now I was here in another strange situation. I said to myself, It doesn't mattter what happens now. It really doesn't. If I die, I don't care. If I live, it would not matter. But I took a spark of hope from those black ladies in religious garb. They were so enthusiastic about helping me.

I said, "I am a junkie. I'm a drug fiend. I need dope."

"Not to worry," she said, "We have something now we call methadone."

"What's methadone?" I asked.

"It's a program we're going to put you on tomorrow."

"How can you do it?" I wondered.

The nuns were confident. "We have ways."

"What am I to do?"

"Just stay here and relax. Anything that you want you just ring this bell."

There was a bell on the wall. The jumbo shot of heroin was taking its toll and I was now nodding into my shake. It spilled onto the floor, and on their charming green rug which lay before the fireplace.

"I'm sorry," I muttered.

"Not to be bothered. Someone will clean it up for you."

A Handmaid of Mary in an apron came to clean it up and brought me another milkshake. They were very nice for an order of Roman Catholic nuns. I was very impressed with them and I did get a sense that I could receive help. As unconvinced as I seemed, I had a sense of hope.

In the morning, I received a charming breakfast of toast, grits, and jelly doughnut. But I wanted something more.

"I need another shot of heroin!"

Sister Incarnata reminded me, "Your heroin has been disposed of."

"What do you mean?" I cried.

"Mother Superior disposed of it last night. You know, possessing it is a criminal offence and carries a very harsh penalty. All that heroin you brought into our convent was disposed of."

"Well, I need another shot. Time for more!"

"We don't have any."

So I screamed and raved and ranted. I was going through slight withdrawal already and Sister Euphemia, who happened to be a doctor of medicine, was summoned at once.

"I can't give you anything but a tranquilizer—Thorazine."

"OH!" I screamed.

She said, "I'm not supposed to do this, but I'll give you a shot of morphine. It's unethical, but I understand your pain, your physical pain as well as your mental anguish. It's against my conscience and my oath as a physician, but I think God will protect us. This will help you until we get you to the methadone program later which we arranged." It was sponsored by the Beth Israel Hospital in conjunction with the Harlem Hospital at the clinic on 125th Street, the Lee Building on the ninth floor.

That affected me very much. That really did. That a nun, secondly a woman, and a doctor of medicine, would give me this morphium, morphine as it's called in the States, to relieve my horrible pain. Later that morning, I was taken to the program. They gave me the methadone, which was incredibly strong (all 120 milligrams of it), and I vomited. It was different from heroin. There was none of the euphoria I experienced with heroin, but it satisfied my craving.

The nuns told me I would go there every day to get methadone. I could hardly wait. Then they began the family lecture again. I insisted that I did not want anything to do with my family at this time. There they were: two nuns staring at me, I in my charming lace nightgown underneath a ranch mink coat, with long red hair dangling over my shoulders and tons of make-up on, and they in their coifs, plain and homely. Yet they had tears in their eyes.

One of them said, "You are cared for by the Lord, but your family also cares about you. We're going to set up a physical examination for you and perhaps then you will decide to let us contact your family."

"I ought to let you know something," I said.

"Yes, Margo?"

"I'm a drag queen."

"Well, we won't discuss that. It doesn't matter what you are. Man, woman, drag queen—you're a child of God."

"How sporting of you, Sister, dear Sister. How very sporting of you to make that statement."

She looked at me pleadingly. "Please let me call your mother."

I hesitated a moment, but then I wrote my mother's phone number for her. They were on the phone before I knew it, and came running back to announce how very happy my mother was to hear from them. It was great news for my mother.

"Your mother is quite anxious to see you," Sister Incarnata said. "She'd like you at home now that you're on this program."

I said, "I don't want to go home."

She talked me into it.

HOME AGAIN

25

SO I WENT home, back to Forest Hills Gardens, and back into the pattern of being watched like a hawk and treated like a human being, even if Mummy continued to give me a hard time for my less-than-conformist lifestyle. From 1969 to 1976, I was taking methadone every day, then every other day, then three times a week, and finally once a week. For the first year on the program, I was very uncertain, understandably quite vulnerable. I gradually became mentally stronger during the second year on the program thanks to a wonderful and charming counselor named Ruth Roister. I was her baby and she was my guiding light. She would say to me, "Methadone is like heroin. It's not good for you. It's gonna destroy you the same way heroin did. We have to gradually decrease the doses until finally we can withdraw them altogether. Then you will be healthy and free."

I was down to two and a half milligrams a week—they didn't get any smaller. Living a low-key existence, a recluse of sorts, I read an incredible amount of literature, but lacked a creative spirit. After all that time hibernating in Harlem, I enthusiastically embraced books, reading two or three a day, and enriching my mind with material from assorted magazines and newspapers. I would read everything cover-to-cover—letters to the editor, editor's notes, articles, advertisements—anxious for it all. I read every journal, manual, instruction booklet for every appliance in the house! I simply could not get enough! I lived a quiet, uneventful life for years in the spacious and lovely confines of Forest Hills Gardens.

In 1976, I had my last dose of methadone. I've been drug-free since. It felt good to be saved. I still longed for the lifestyle with which I had become familiar, yet I indulged in my fun with a limited appetite. I now knew not to go too far. I could stop myself when enough was becoming too much. I revived my friendships with Joey, Deanna, and Adrienne. I saw less and less of the crazier queens—surely, they were never my friends, but merely partners in crime.

The treatments were going well. Although it was an addiction to end an addiction, I felt reassured by its proven medical adequacy. Adventures continued, though less frequently. It was a year of living quietly amongst the elite in Forest Hills Gardens. When I ventured across the river to Manhattan, it was to visit friends who had little or no affiliation with drugs, people like "Low Low" Lola (although no one was like Lola) Betinis, an instructor at Hunter College by day and a wild and fun-loving socialite by night. Her father was a prestigious surgeon and she used what he freely offered her to treat her friends. I met the exotic Brazilian temptress, Josara Maria Krause, whose mother was a princess married to an escaped Nazi war criminal. Josara lived with Bill Mulcahy, a retired stockbroker, generous with his fortune. During their outrageous parties, Josara was a show-off when it came to emphasizing her bombshell physique.

Joey Kane, who was occasionally Kora, was with me one day when we ran into Judy Garland at Gray's drug store on 50th Street. We were browsing through the cosmetics, excited about a brand new product from Max Factor, a creamy rose pancake make-up, when I eyed a small, frail woman. She was thin as a stick. I recognized her as Judy Garland. She turned to me and said, "I bet that's becoming on you." I thanked her and noticed that she did not look at all well. Indeed, she confessed she was feeling rather ill. Joey and I invited her for a drink. "Would that help?" we asked. "Not hardly," she said. Well, we paid for our cosmetics, and Judy followed us to Joey's place on 69th Street off Central Park West. It was there that we gave her a mild sedative to ease her pain. She ended up staying for three days—not bothering to bathe or use make-up.

On the fourth day, she took Joey and me over to see Martha Raye, who had a penthouse on 72nd Street off West End Avenue. Martha Raye was drunk and disorderly, and our party continued for a few more days.

Later that week, Mark Herron showed up and told Judy she was looking terrible.

TALLULAH BANKHEAD

26

I STILL have Tallulah's Hadassah Woman of the Year pin. It has her name, the award, and the year "1956" written on it in Gothic letters. It's gold. A Southern woman, she had fought for civil rights for all—women and blacks included—throughout her life.

And I have her lighter at home, and her checkbook, too. I met her through a friend of mine called Chuck Mitchell, who was from Hartford, Connecticut—blond, very handsome, and homosexual. Tallulah adored him. I met her in 1969. A few weeks later she went to the hospital and died.

Chuck Mitchell took me to meet her one day at her apartment on East 57th Street; the apartment had a *porte cochère* right near Sutton Place. It was a lovely building right on the corner. She was wheezing then, gasp gasp gasp; she had emphysema. She took Seconals by the handful, and when Chuck tried to take them away from her, she beat him with her fists.

She would scream at her servants, "Run my bath!" Her bath had to be just the right temperature and dosed with Vitabath, a marvelous source of rejuvenation that I was then prompted to use and continue to do so to this day.

After imbibing a few, I saw her lighter on the table and I palmed it. It was gold, an Alfred Dunhill. At one point I excused myself from the room. When I came back she said to me: "You are a Methadonian." I had a bottle of Methadone in there. It was my weekend supply. "How do you know?" I asked. She told me she looked through my handbag while I was out of the room.

"I see you have my lighter, too," she said. "That's all right. Take it for a souvenir. I have plenty more in the closet." Apparently, she put things out on purpose, expecting them to be stolen. She called it "trucking privileges." She knew people were taking advantage of her. Pathetic, really.

She was at death's door. She died a week later. She was an interesting person. She had her ways.

JACKIE CURTIS

27

WHEN you come down to the bottom line, Jackie Curtis was a poor soul. Very talented, but something very basic was lacking. I knew him so well, and I'm very perceptive about these things.

In this period I was on methadone treatment, going to clubs and hanging out, but I wasn't doing any soliciting. Now, my life has had a complete turn-around. I whored, lady/gentlemen that I was. I did receive, ultimately, redemption. Of course, one can always say, Oh my God, I'm not ashamed of anything I've done, but I regret many things. But I did things because I had to, at the time I was taking heroin—robbing men, deceiving, etc., etc., but I'm not ashamed of it. I had to do it at the time. I had no choice.

In a way I experienced a certain religious awakening, although I did not conform to religious practices, such as going to churches, or to Zen Buddhism which, as you know, was very popular then. I pray even now to God. I believe in God. I am a lapsed member of the Roman Church. I only go to the Mass once a year, on February 8, for Mary Stuart, a special Mass said on the anniversary of her death. I give a donation to them to say the Mass—at St. Thomas More, St. Ignatius Loyola, St. Patrick's Cathedral. In the Lady Chapel at St. Patrick's Cathedral. It was in the papers.

I marked my time by doing a lot of scholarly work. I really got into it. For four years I wrote essays, mostly on historical data. This is when I got to know Jackie Curtis, Andy Warhol, and Taylor Mead.

I met Jackie at my hairdresser's place. We got to know each other very well. I would spend weekends with him, and when he had shows, I would help him with them. We would stay up for nights on end, telling each other our life stories. But Jackie was sick in the head. He was like Marilyn Monroe in her prime. He was a megalomaniac, uncheckable. He thought he was a genius. He would say, "I am Jackie Curtis. I am a superstar." I would say to him, "You're the queen of megalomania." I was the only one that Jackie would listen to. I said to him, "You haven't done a thing in ten years. You're not a superstar. You were never a superstar. You're nothing."

I got him to work and rewrite the play "Glamor, Glory and Gold." I never got any credit. It's always a devious thing that way; mostly my work. Jackie Curtis was a plagiarist. Some of what is known as his work is my work and he claimed it. Most of it was horrible . . . but "Glamor, Glory and Gold" is good.

Concurrently I got to know Andy Warhol. He was terrified of me, for some reason. Andy started snapping pictures of me, everywhere I went. So one day I got fed up. I walked up to Andy Warhol at Max's Kansas City, in the early 70s, and I grabbed his camera, and said, "Look, Miss Warhol, you piece of shit, enough is enough. If you want to take my picture you ask me, lady or gentleman or whatever I am." And I took the film and the camera and threw them on the floor. He was deathly afraid of people. He cringed and his bodyguards cringed too; I was so adamant, you might say. And ever after that, at an opening, he would say, "Excuse me, Margo, can I take pictures of you?" And I'd pose. I did get that rotten bitch to ask.

In 1969, when I had just been released from the drug heroin and was on the methadone program, Jackie Curtis brought me to a party at the Factory, which was on 14th Street at Union Square, and there I met Ondine, Taylor Mead, Holly Woodlawn, and Candy Darling. Holly Woodlawn was one of Andy's stars, a drag queen. Candy Darling, who is now dead, was very famous. Died of cancer. Had the breasts enlarged. I never had any physical enlargements. It's only fat. Too much tummy too. Never thought for a moment about having any kind of operation. My mental health is pretty good that way.

150

So I met Taylor Mead just casually. In the 70s I got to know him better, and then we had readings together, poetry readings, at various places. We're very good friends, very close. He's very good to me. He's done a lot for me.

Andy robbed Jackie Curtis. Jackie was in *Women in Revolt*, and several of his films, and Andy didn't pay him. He never paid anyone. He gave them drugs and amphetamines and whatever they wanted, and locked them in The Factory. They were there for days until the film was made. He bolted the doors so they couldn't get out. A little pocket money, and all the drugs they wanted he acquired for them. Heroin. Amphetamines. For *Women in Revolt*, Jackie Curtis got $163. At the most. All the drugs and booze they wanted, and boys. He would acquire young men. For that purpose only, to fuck 'em or suck 'em, whatever, from sixteen to twenty-two, young and foolish and impressed by Andy Warhol.

Andy Warhol, when you come down to the bottom line, with all his good deeds, and attending the Holy Sacrifice of the Mass every day— he used to go to church every morning, and give money to the Church, loads of money to the Church, to the poor—well, he was an unscrupulous bastard, and when you come down to it, he was a charlatan. Really, in my opinion. Of course, I'm a lunatic. But he was a devious charlatan. Look at poor Jackie Curtis. A hundred and sixty dollars for *Women in Revolt*. He used and abused.

Ondine was the one actor who got anything out of Andy Warhol. Out of the whole group. Ondine is of a certain age. About fifty-two. An actor. American born, Yugoslavian parents. He has the rights to one or two of Andy's movies. He was able to get Andy in a vulnerable moment, the only one that got ahead of Andy.

Andy left his brother $100,000. His older brother works in the steel mills. And he set up a foundation for the arts. God knows what it's going to do.

MARY, QUEEN OF SCOTS

28

THE EARLY 1970s brought me many new friends. I teamed up with Tom Weigel, poet and founder of *Tangerine* magazine. We continue to work on many projects together, especially The Mary Stuart Society functions, something very close to my heart. We honor the memory of Mary, Queen of Scots in order to further the efforts to recognize and pay tribute to the arts as the late Mary Stuart did. Annually, we host a tea party at a distinguished meeting place where we read aloud selected poems and prose pieces which either directly or indirectly praise the late and tragic queen.

We have a very special roster of members which grows in number every year. We also hope to eventually see the passing of the Equal Rights Amendment for women. And now the Royal Stuart Society of England wants me to merge with them. They're very influential. They are lunatics too. They don't know anything about my lifestyle. They think I'm a woman. When I'm in drag, most people think I'm a woman. No one ever asks. If they asked, I would tell them, but what you see is what you get. No one has ever asked me. In the right places, I mean. I've never considered a sex change. Too radical.

People's attitudes toward everything have changed, actually. The world has grown up. In all classes. Even the working classes, the welfare class, the public charges all over the world have become more liberal.

Gay rights and all that radical bullshit, I'm not into all that humbug. I don't watch most parades. What for? When you come down to the bottom line, people are people. They're either going to be nice and decent, or they're going to be rotten bastards. You can't change them. It's been this way since time immemorial, and it will always be this way.

ANDY ON THE BLOCK

29

ON THE 25th of April 1988, which was a Monday, I had a reading at the
St. Mark's Poetry Project with Penny Arcade at eight o'clock. The same
night I was invited to attend a viewing of Andy Warhol's effects that were
going on sale at Sotheby's—not his personal works of art, but things he
had collected. He amassed a lot of garbage—urinals, cookie jars, some
nice 1930s dishes, some nice early 20th Century marble, but a lot of
kitsch. The antiques were not antique, they were reproductions, made
after 1900.

I was wearing a 1920s brocaded velvet coat, a marvelous piece. It
was my mother's. Some woman came over and told me she thought the
coat was fabulous, and asked where she could buy it. I told her I stole it
from Andy Warhol. She laughed and walked away.

Baird Jones, a man about town, came up to me and informed me
I had been speaking to Madonna, the singer and actress.

Then this singular-looking man drifted by. I admired his stance.
He stood so upright. He was of a certain age. He had a mustache and
silver hair. He caught my eye as I was looking at him, and came over and
introduced himself as Thomas Hoving. He glanced at my name tag.
"Margo Howard. Do I know you?" I told him no. "Oh, well, I thought
perhaps we met." I said we had not. "That's a beautiful jacket you're
wearing," he said. I thanked him. He asked if it was a vintage piece; I said
it was. "Are you here perhaps to buy something from Andy Warhol's

personal effects?" I told him I wouldn't buy anything that Andy Warhol collected. I thought he was despicable. He said, "So do a lot of people. Even now that he's dead. But why do you?"

You don't speak ill of the dead. However. Andy had done a lot of my friends out of what they deserved—like Taylor Mead, and Jackie Curtis. They did movies with him and he hardly paid them at all, unless one counts drugs and a very few dollars. I mentioned this to Tom, who is former director of the Metropolitan Museum of Art.

He said he had heard that, and asked me if I was in the arts. So I went on, in my megalomania. I said, "I'm an actress, a playwright, a composer of music. I'm a painter of sorts." I went on and on and on.

He said, "Are you doing anything now?"

"Yes, I am. I have a book coming out in November."

"Oh? On what subject?"

"On me."

"May I ask what it's called?"

"Certainly. It's called, Tom, *I Was A White Slave in Harlem*."

His face was very stoic, very calm. He said, "Oh." I said, "O is a big round letter." He said, "Yes, it is." I said, "It's not what you think. I was not a slave to bondage or sado-masochism, or a slave to black lust as a white woman. It's about being a slave to drugs, to heroin, and my eventual recovery after living with a drug dealer in Harlem."

He said, "Very interesting." Then he said, "Oh, Brooke dear, come over here, I want you to meet Margo Howard." "Howard-Howard," I corrected him.

"Howard-Howard. She has written a book about Harlem."

This was to Brooke Astor. She said, "Oh, really? I do a lot of social work uptown. I'm a volunteer in a settlement house in Harlem."

"It is not a book about Harlem, Mrs. Astor. This is a book about me living in Harlem."

Again the face did not move, and she went, "Hmmmmm." I said, "Hmmmmm means an awful lot. Allow me to explain. It's a biography of my life. It's about redemption. It's about me living in Harlem with one of America's greatest entrepreneurs in drug sales. I am a former heroin addict and it's about my life as an addict." She said, "May I shake your hand?"

She said, "I have been working with young mothers who are drug addicts in Harlem. MARY!" she called, and she said, "This is Mrs. Albert Lasker. This wonderful young lady . . ." I said, "Well, I'm not really a young lady. I'm a drag queen." She said, "What?" I said, "I'm a man in women's clothes." And she went, "Oh, you look so beautiful and real." I said, "That's very sporting of you to say. Thank you, Mrs. Astor." She said, "Oh, call me Brooke, please."

She was well-preserved. You couldn't tell how old she was. She could be fifty or she could be seventy. She had a face so tight you know she had five face lifts. The other one was Mrs. Albert Lasker, who puts all the flowers in Park Avenue every year. And Brooke said of me, "Oh, she's so wonderful. She's so wonderful. She wrote a book about her former life."

And they all clustered around me, all the grande dames of New York. And there I was, holding court. A photographer came in and Tom Hoving said: "Willy, get a picture of us. Will you hold my arm, please?" And he announced, "Her name is Margo Howard-Howard and she has a biography coming out in November."

Hoving was very nice to me, but I suddenly looked at the time. "Oh my God, it's seven thirty and I have an appointment downtown at eight o'clock to read excerpts from my book," I said. "Oh, I was going to invite you to have dinner," Tom said. "We'd love to take you to dinner." But I said I had to go, and he told me to use his car. So I went to the Poetry Project in a limo.

Andy's ghost would not have smiled. Andy was a cocksucker, a venal man. He was not a nice person. That's the last gratuity I got from Andy Warhol—a round pint bottle of Absolut, a party favor from Sotheby's.

THE CHURCH

30

MOST of the archbishops of New York—the last four, who were cardinals—now we don't talk about the dead, but Cardinal Spellman was an old closet queen. Personally I never saw him sucking a cock or whatever he was given to doing. But I heard rumors in the homophile world that he was called "Fanny" Spellman. That he liked "seafood." Sailors. For a soldier, one would say "K-rations." Well, old Fanny, prince of the church, was gossiped about all over town. Then the late archbishop of New York, Terrence Cardinal Cooke, Miss Terry, rumors also, but then fags are such gossips. They say he didn't die from leukemia, that he died from AIDS.

As for O'Connor, I met him. I sent him a lovely letter when he became the Archbishop of New York. My humbug way of writing letters. I sent him a letter at the Chancery saying, "We of the Mary Stuart Society are praying for you as New York's new spiritual leader. You're in our prayers." I got a lovely card back, and when he became a cardinal there was a reception for him in New York and I was invited and I went and met him. I looked very ladylike. I went there with Jacqueline Durstin, who's now dead. She was a French princess. Jacqueline de Bourbon. She was on our letterhead. She was the secretary and treasurer of the Mary Stuart Society. She was Mrs. Roy S. Durstin, formerly Her Royal Highness Princess Jacqueline de Boubon. She was married to Roy Durstin, whose father founded Barton, Barton, Durstin & Osborne, BBD & O. Advertising. We went together. She knew my story. Some of the old ladies in the

Society were convinced that I was a woman. One of them once said of me, "Well, she's awfully tall, and her voice sounds like a man's sometimes." Jane Emmet, who is a very old lady, whose brother, now dead, William Temple Emmet, was a john of mine, and whose home I visited several times when no one was there—she was convinced she knew me when I was a young lady in the forties.

I got old ladies to join the Mary Stuart Society by going through the Social Register picking out names. You could tell how old they were by what class they were in at school. I wrote to them and I got about 150 members. We had teas at the Carlyle and at the Plaza. That's when it was very small. Then Jacqueline died. Two princesses died that year, and nobody came because so many members had died that year. I lost two princesses, five members. Every member pays the minimum, $80 a year, you know. We have meetings.

I knew that Jane Emmet's mother was a famous suffragette and a very strange woman. As a matter of fact, I met her once when I was in woman's clothes and she thought I was a woman too. Years and years ago, this is, in her beautiful home in Stony Brook. She had a huge estate. She was a tyrant, very much like my mother but older. I said to Jane, "We've met before at your brother's apartment at nine-something Fifth Avenue." I went there one time with her brother, William. He said, "Oh, thank God Christopher isn't here." Christopher was the other brother, who died. He was the head of the International Rescue Committee. So I said, "Oh, your brother's lovely flat on Fifth Avenue." It was a whole floor, it was there from 1922 or something. And a beautiful house at Stony Brook, Long Island, which was built by some famous architect. I met the mother one time. We were at Easthampton at the Maidstone Club for a weekend, and we stopped off to visit her. She was a monstrously heavy woman. She lived to be 100 years old. And he said, "Oh, Mother, this is Margaret Howard-Howard." "Howard," she said, "I know the Howards. How are you a Howard-Howard?" I said, "Well, Mrs. Emmet, I'm a Howard by birth, and then I married my fourth cousin, who also had the surname Howard." "Oh," she said, "that sounds strange. You should have just one Howard. But you can do what you want."

So I said, "Oh, I met your charming mother at her lovely home at

Stony Brook." And she said, "Oh yes, you knew Mummy." I said yes, she was so wonderful with women's rights. "Oh, women's rights," she said. "Women's rights mean nothing."

I had her to tea for the Mary Stuart Society in the Carlyle Hotel in '84. There were over 100 people there. Princess Zu-Weid, who died in my presence, was there. And someone said, "Margo Howard is rather strange. She's very mannish. Who is she? I've never heard of her. I think she's an imposter of some sort." And Jane Emmet said, "How dare you speak so of Margo Howard-Howard? I remember her when she was young and lovely. It's hard to believe she's that age." Jane Emmet said to me, "I remember when you came out, at the Ritz-Carlton Hotel. It was during the war. In was 1943. Wasn't it?" I just smiled. By saying nothing, I convinced her that she attended my debut at the Ritz-Carlton Hotel in 1943. "Oh no, I attended her debut in 1943, at the Christmas Grosvenor Ball." She was gaga. She'd said, "I don't recall meeting you." I said, "Well, it was in the summer, and it was a terribly warm day at your brother's Fifth Avenue digs." And she said, "Oh, yes, of course it was. That was in 1949, wasn't it?" And I just smiled. It convinced her.

But about Princess Karl-Victor Zu-Weid, who died in my presence. A German princess, but she was American. Her own name was Eileen Johnson, and Eileen Johnson did not handle her liquor well. She was very beautiful, she was in her 60s, she was living in the Stanhope Hotel on Fifth Avenue, and she knew my story. She used to say, "Laura's no good." Laura de Copet, her daughter, is an old girlfriend of Leo Castelli. Laura de Copet is over forty years old, very beautiful. She has an Electra complex. Very sweet. As a matter of fact she called me up the other day. "I saw you on Page Six. Come over and have tea." Her mother was a very lovely woman, every summer she'd go to London to live in Claridge's. Anyway, Eileen Johnson lived in the Stanhope Hotel and drank like a fish. Several times I had to pick her up, she was falling down drunk. She took barbituates too. Very charming. I would visit her. She would give me a white envelope with $500 in it. She'd say, "Buy yourself a dress. I'm sick of that tweed suit. It's thirty years old." I'd say, "It was my mother's." She'd say, "It looks it. Buy yourself a new one." And she'd give me money each time I'd go there, because she was a very lonely woman. But very nice when she was sober.

She knew the story. She'd say, "Are you a lesbian or are you a man in woman's clothes, a transvestite?" I'd say, "I don't like the word transvestite. I'm a drag queen. I'm not going to lie to you because you know me." She'd say, "Yeah." She was a Johnson & Johnson from Princeton, New Jersey.

I went to visit her in November two years ago, in the afternoon. She was having a drink, and she was drunk as a skunk. She opened a drawer and took some red pills, Seconal, about four of them. I said, "You shouldn't do that." She said, "Aw, shut the hell up." And she drank a tall glass full of Absolut. I said, "My God, how can you drink that without any mix?" "It's like water to me," she said. She drank that, finished it, put it down, sat down and just closed her eyes. I said, "Eileen! Eileen!" I called downstairs and said, "Will you please send up a doctor?" She died in my presence. Just keeled back in the chair. She looked very peaceful, very beautiful. She had platinum blonde hair. She was 63.

Princess Karl-Victor Zu-Weid. Her husband, Karl-Victor Zu-Weid, was an old German homophile who was tried at Nuremberg in the Second World War. He was in charge of the Nazi Red Cross in Germany from 1933.

Back to the O'Connor reception. Jacqueline said to him, "Your Eminence, I'm the secretary and treasurer of the Mary Stuart Society, and this is our founder and chairperson, Margo Howard." I was so honored. He never had any idea. I came across very quietly. "Hello," I said. "How do you do?" Sometimes less is more. I dress very respectably. Low voice, low and quiet. Some of these society women and horse women from New Jersey, they boom and they have shoulders like football players. Next to them I look tiny, I look demure. Half the bona fide women look like men in women's clothes.

I prefer to be called a drag queen. A transvestite is a medical term. Doctors and psychiatrists use that. A transvestite is a person who could be heterosexual or homosexual or asexual, who receives a sexual thrill from wearing women's attire. I don't really feel comfortable in a dress, and it's not a thrill. It's just something that I got into for self-gratification, sexual

162

or mental. I happen to have some feminine genes which I think over-ride my male ones. I look better in women's clothes than in men's clothes. My softness is a woman's grace.

It's a matter of acceptance. I'm more accepted by many people when I'm in woman's clothes than in man's clothes. People look at me and they say, "Is that a girlish boy, or is that a boyish girl?" It's what I call my ungendered look. I have an ungendered appearance. When I put on the dress, I look more presentable. I really have become, in a half century's time, a grande dame.

REFLECTION

31

I DIDN'T write this book to shock or to appall people. This book is not about corruption—getting away with something, doing something and getting away with it, ha-ha-ha, having a mink coat. My life has been sordid and sick, not a healthy existence. But in the end if I, in the middle of my life, could accomplish something, could redeem myself—if I could give up heroin, and stay off heroin for almost twenty years, why can't someone else? Why can't some twenty-one-year-old or twenty-two-year-old college student do the thing if I could and can do it? There's no such thing as the impossible.

I've been entirely off drugs for twenty years—although I had a little problem with pills, stimulants, weight reduction pills which I don't take any more.

I always exercise. I jog in Forest Park in Queens, every morning, for about a mile, with my poodle barking and yapping by my side.

I'm very quiet and reserved these days. I live with my sister the spinster. She's adored by all. She's a very kind lady. Everyone tells her how wonderful she is. She came to my show at the World. She's very giving and accepting, whereas my other sisters are very conservative. But I survived them.

These days, I'm acting. I take a class once every two weeks with a private drama coach in the village. And I write. I've done a lot of historical research, particularly on the sixteenth century. And I have my doll collection. I started collecting dolls in about 1970, after my experience with drugs. I have forty-four dolls now. I bought them in antique shops, when it wasn't very chic to collect them, and now they're worth quite a lot. The timing was right. The Empress Eugénie doll, which is a Jumeau—by a famous French doll maker—is worth thousands now. It was made in 1862, and I have the papers on it. There are about five or six left in the world.

QUEEN TO QUEEN

32

FOR THE 400th Anniversary of the death of Mary Stuart, I decided that I would fly to the U.K. and pay my respects directly at the grave. I wrote a letter to the Royal Stuart Society of England to see if there would be a special commemoration ceremony. Gloria Talbot Vessey of the R.S.S. sent her reply on 22 January, 1987 with the following information:

The Royal Stuart Society's Commemorations will, in fact, take place on Friday, 6 February, as follows:

2:30 p.m.   Prayers & wreath laying in the royal tomb in Westminster Abbey.

6:30 p.m.   Latin Mass in the Domestic Chapel, The Society of Jesus, 114 Mount, St., London W1 by kind invitation of Monsignor A. N. Gilbey.

7–7:30 p.m.   Short reception in the parish hall, 114 Mount St.

7:30 p.m.   Annual Mary, Queen of Scots Lecture to be given by the Reverend Francis Edwards SJ FSA on "Mary, Queen of Scots 100 years ago: almost a saint or still a sinner?" We should be happy to see you at any or all of these events.

You may also be interested to know that the Bishop of Northampton will be celebrating Mass to mark the quarter century in Fotheringhay Parish Church on Sunday, 8 February, at 3 p.m. Some members of this society will be attending.

Westminster Abbey was to be the highlight of the event, and the short reception at the Society headquarters at 114 Mount Street with Monsignor A. N. Gilbey, or Lord Gilbey, I was sure would be quite a thrill as well.

I checked into the hotel in London, dressed in men's attire, on 5th February. A bit of jet lag followed, but John Perkurny, who accompanied me on this voyage, began to set my hair. The next day, I got all dolled up in my grand tweed suit, had the bellboy call a cab for us, and drove off to Westminster Abbey where Mary Stuart rests in peaceful slumber in the Henry VII Chapel. I announced myself to the verger: "I'm Margo Howard-Howard and I'm here for the Royal Stuart Society's Memorial for the Scottish Queen."

He said, "They're at the information desk. Go there and announce yourself. They're expecting you, Margo Howard-Howard from America?"

"Yes," I said and thanked him.

At the information desk, I announced myself again with my intentions. He directed me to the Dean's Parlour, a small sitting room to the side. Right away, I knew who was who. A rolypoly fat man in a black robe managed a weak smile.

"I'm Margo Howard-Howard," I told him, "and I am here for the Memorial Service. I was invited as a guest of the Royal Stuart Society."

He said, "Oh my dear, I'm so glad that you made yourself known. I'm St. Albans. How do you do?"

I said, "How do you do, Duke?"

I knew the Duke of St. Albans was governing general of the R.S.S. He said, "Call me Charles."

I said, "Well, if I call you Charles, you have to call me Margo."

He smiled, bowed graciously, and said, "Let me inform you,

Margo, in case you don't know, that the Queen will be here for the festivities. Would you like to be presented?"

"Well," I said, "I don't know if I rate being presented. I'm not sure if I deserve that honor."

He said, "Oh, of course you do. You came all the way from America. Most certainly!"

It was, lo and behold, 2:22. That gave us only seven minutes until we would lay the wreath. It took exactly that much time to walk to the tomb. When we got there, the clergyman announced that Her Majesty had arrived. He instructed us on what to do when she entered the chapel. We were to walk ten to fifteen feet behind the royal party at all times. We would walk in the pattern: one, two, one, two. Wow, I thought, it was just like the army.

Along she came with her entourage. The Dean of the Abbey ahead of her, and two clergymen, one carrying a wreath, the other a giant crucifix, both dressed in layers of black robes. I along with about thirty members of the Royal Stuart Society followed behind. We all crowded into the corridor which was not only quite tiny, but under heavy restoration, the scaffolding obstructing all but the actual tomb.

The Queen stood silent. Then one of the clergymen dropped to his knees and began praying in Latin. The other dropped down as well as they both recited the Lord's Prayer and the Hail Mary. They then stood upright and announced. "We are here to commemorate the 400th Anniversary of the murder of Mary Stuart." They were fanatic about stressing the word "murder" rather than "execution". They said a few more prayers and the man holding the wreath handed it to the Queen. She placed it gently on the carving of Mary Stuart which was underneath the statue. The wreath was made entirely out of white lilies and a huge ribbon displayed the royal crests of France, England, and Scotland. The Queen curtsied right down to the floor and then kissed the coat of arms on the ribbon. She stepped back and there was a period of tranquility. All the members of the Royal Stuart Society, one at a time, bowed formally to the Queen and kissed the ribbon just as she had. I was amongst the last in turn.

The Duke of St. Albans approached me. "Margo Howard-Howard,

I'd like to present you now." Then, just as the Queen was ready to leave, he said, "Your Majesty, I'd like to present Margo Howard-Howard. She has come all the way from New York in America to be with us today to pay honor to the memory of the Scots' Queen."

The Queen seemed genuinely delighted and offered her hand, "Margo Howard, how do you do? How are you feeling?"

I curtsied, a court curtsy—I touched one knee to the floor—and I said, "Quite fine, your Majesty."

She said, "I just want to thank you personally for honoring my favorite ancestor by founding The Mary Stuart Society." She smiled, and walked off. A moment later, she turned around and said, "Thank you once again."

I watched her walk away. We had to wait, oh, until she was ten or fifteen feet away, but I stood there until she was out of sight. She's a rather nice lady, said one queen of the other.

CHRONOLOGY AND FAMILY TREE

CHRONOLOGY

1935: Born Robert Chanler Hesse, Singapore.

1942: Left Singapore. Father killed by Japanese. Fled to Bombay, then Chile. Trip through South America by hired car.

1946: Moved to Forest Hills Gardens. Attended Kew Forest Country Day School: skipped ahead of class several times.

1947: Entered Portsmouth Priory—now the Abbey School, Rhode Island.

1951: Entered Georgetown University. Acknowledged own homosexuality.

1953: Met James Dean.

1955: Graduated from Georgetown, major in history. Moved to New York. Married to and divorced from daughter of "chewing gum mogul." Worked as teacher; dismissed due to violent confrontation with students. Committed to West Hills Sanitarium.

1957: Adopted name of Margo Howard-Howard. Initial drug experimentation.

1959: Met "Saul Hite," an English Jewish gentleman with a wooden leg. Met Nina, the crazy Russian lady. Began using hard drugs and hustling to support drug habit.

1964: Met and seduced by Leroy "Nicky" Barnes. Lived with him until 1969.

1969: Saved by the Handmaids of Mary.

1969–76: Methadone treatment. Recovery from heroin addiction. Met Andy Warhol, Jackie Curtis.

1982: Mother died January 6th. Formed the Mary Stuart Society.

1983: Published in *Tangerine* magazine. First tapes for *White Slave* recorded with Tom Weigel.

1984: Began work on autobiography with Abbe Michaels. Met John Cardinal O'Connor, Archbishop of New York.

1985: Penny Arcade begins impersonations of Margo for stage.

1987: Met the Queen.

CHANLER FAMILY TREE

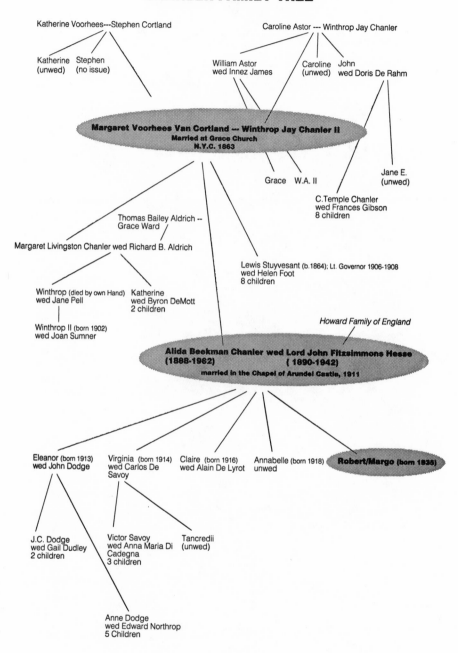

Katherine Voorhees---Stephen Cortland

Katherine (unwed) Stephen (no issue)

Caroline Astor --- Winthrop Jay Chanler

William Astor wed Innez James

Caroline (unwed) John wed Doris De Rahm

Margaret Voorhees Van Cortland --- Winthrop Jay Chanler II
Married at Grace Church
N.Y.C. 1863

Grace W.A. II

C.Temple Chanler
wed Frances Gibson
8 children

Jane E. (unwed)

Thomas Bailey Aldrich --
Grace Ward

Margaret Livingston Chanler wed Richard B. Aldrich

Lewis Stuyvesant (b.1864); Lt. Governor 1906-1908
wed Helen Foot
8 children

Winthrop (died by own Hand)
wed Jane Pell

Katherine
wed Byron DeMott
2 children

Winthrop II (born 1902)
wed Joan Sumner

Howard Family of England

Alida Beekman Chanler wed Lord John Fitzsimmons Hesse
(1888-1962)   (1890-1942)
married in the Chapel of Arundel Castle, 1911

Eleanor (born 1913)
wed John Dodge

Virginia (born 1914)
wed Carlos De
Savoy

Claire (born 1916)
wed Alain De Lyrot

Annabelle (born 1918)
unwed

Robert/Margo (born 1935)

J.C. Dodge
wed Gail Dudley
2 children

Victor Savoy
wed Anna Maria Di
Cadegna
3 children

Tancredii
(unwed)

Anne Dodge
wed Edward Northrop
5 Children

AFTERWORD

ON THE verge of pulling off one final "deception," as she would have put it, a few weeks before the release of this book, Margo Howard-Howard died suddenly. Many of those who spoke to her in the months preceding her death remarked on the enthusiasm with which she looked forward to the hard-won publication of her "memoirs."

We learned shortly thereafter that much, if not most, of what is written here is fictional. Margo is not, in fact, a nephew of the "Marquis of Shropshire." Her family did not flee the Japanese in World War II (she was born in New York City); she may or may not have had encounters with James Dean, Truman Capote and Leroy "Nicky" Barnes. That said, she did accomplish a great deal in reality—meeting the Queen, surviving drug addiction, founding the Mary Stuart Society . . . She created a life and a history—complete with chronology and detailed family tree—instead of merely acquiring them.

Four Walls Eight Windows

Books from

FOUR WALLS EIGHT WINDOWS

Algren, Nelson. **NEVER COME MORNING.** pb: $7.95

Anderson, Sherwood. **THE TRIUMPH OF THE EGG.** pb: $8.95

Brodsky, Michael. **X IN PARIS.** pb: $9.95

Brodsky, Michael. **XMAN.** cl: $21.95 pb: $11.95

Codrescu, Andrei, ed.
AMERICAN POETRY SINCE 1970: UP LATE.
cl: $23.95 pb: $12.95

Dubuffet, Jean.
ASPHYXIATING CULTURE AND OTHER WRITINGS. cl: $17.95

Howard-Howard, Margo (with Abbe Michaels).
I WAS A WHITE SLAVE IN HARLEM. pb: $12.95

Johnson, Phyllis, and Martin, David, Eds.
**FRONTLINE SOUTHERN AFRICA:
DESTRUCTIVE ENGAGEMENT.**
cl: $23.95 pb: $14.95

Null, Gary.
**THE EGG PROJECT:
GARY NULL'S COMPLETE GUIDE TO GOOD EATING.**
cl: $21.95 pb: $12.95

Santos, Rosario, ed.
**AND WE SOLD THE RAIN: CONTEMPORARY FICTION
FROM CENTRAL AMERICA.**
cl: $18.95 pb: $9.95

Sokolov, Sasha. **A SCHOOL FOR FOOLS.** pb: $9.95

Wasserman, Harvey.
HARVEY WASSERMAN'S HISTORY OF THE UNITEDSTATES.
pb: $6.95

Weber, Brom, ed.
**O MY LAND, MY FRIENDS:
THE SELECTED LETTERS OF HART CRANE.**
cl: $21.95 pb:$12.95

To order, send check or money order to Four Walls Eight Windows, P.O. Box 548, Village Station, New York, NY 10014, or call 1-800-835-2246, ext. 123. Add $2.50 postage and handling for the first book and 50¢ for each additional book.